Fast Boat
Navigation

ALSO IN THE MOTORBOATS MONTHLY SERIES

Practical Motor Cruising
Dag Pike
ISBN 0 229 11827 5

The first title in the series breaks new ground in that it avoids the formal approach and instead takes the motor cruiser owner (both novice and experienced) by the hand to show them the ropes of *practical* motorboat handling and management.

Distilling 40 years of experience in all types of powered craft from motor cruisers to offshore powerboats and even lifeboats, Dag Pike explains how planning and displacement boats behave, how to handle them skilfully in all conditions in harbour, on rivers and at sea, describes what makes them tick and advises how to get the best from them.

Pike explains that the key to good boat handling is preparation and planning – and having something in reserve for when things go wrong. Knowing your boat, learning about the weather, the sea and how it behaves, matching the speed to the conditions and knowing how to navigate effectively will all contribute to help you become a proficient and safe motorboat skipper – and, most importantly, to enjoy it!

Fast Boats and Rough Seas
Dag Pike
ISBN 0 229 11840 2

This is a more advanced follow-up to *Practical Motor Cruising*, and is designed to explain advanced handling techniques for fast boats. With a very practical emphasis, Pike covers high speed handling as well as operating techniques in rough weather, all based on personal experience.

Fast Boats and Rough Seas begins with an analysis of how waves are formed and their effect on the boat. Pike then looks at hull shape as related to speed and seaworthiness, controlling the boat, crew comfort, navigation

under difficult conditions, power requirements, equipment and fittings for high speed, and emergency procedures. Lastly he considers weather changes and describes tactics for avoiding the worst of storm conditions.

Throughout, Pike's approach is wholly practical, as one would expect from such a highly experienced seaman. Even experienced skippers and crew will welcome this book and value its sound advice, from preparation through to emergency procedures.

Marine Inboard Engines: Petrol and Diesel
Loris Goring
ISBN 0 229 11842 9

If you quake at the thought of looking under your engine hatch, this book is the answer to your problems. You may be wondering

- What are the advantages and disadvantages of petrol versus diesel engines?
- What power am I actually buying?
- What addivites are there in a can of engine oil? Should I add more?
- Would I be better with 2 or 4 valve cyclinder heads?
- What electrical problems might I encounter?
- Is an air cooled engine necessarily noisier than water cooled?
- What should I look for when buying a used engine?
- How do electronic ignition systems work?
- What should I do if the engine floods?

Marine Inboard Engines is pitched so that it will neither baffle the newcomer nor bore the old hand, who is sure to learn a few new wrinkles from these pages. Goring gives guidance as to which jobs the amateur can safely undertake – and those which should be left strictly to the professional engineer.

Marine Inboard Engines should enable every owner to spot problems, know when they can be remedied easily, and be able to maintain a petrol or diesel engine to maximise its life and avoid breakdown at sea.

Fast Boat Navigation

DAG PIKE

ADLARD COLES *NAUTICAL*

Published by Adlard Coles *Nautical*
an imprint of A & C Black (Publishers) Ltd
35 Bedford Row, London WC1R 4JH

© Dag Pike 1990

First edition 1990

ISBN 0–229–11859–3

A CIP catalogue record for this book is available from
the British Library.

Printed and bound in Great Britain by
Butler & Tanner Ltd, Frome and London

Contents

Introduction

High speed on the water is no longer the prerogative of the racing boat. Today sports cruisers and patrol boats can top the 40-knot mark. Yet the techniques of navigating at these speeds have tended to rely on the established navigation methods – dead reckoning and visual observation combined with radar where it is available.

With the advent of modern electronics a whole range of new possibilities for fast boat navigation are opened up. Now the techniques can keep up with the speed, although the basics of navigation must not be ignored. The techniques of fast boat navigation to be found in this book are the result of extensive practical experience in a wide variety of fast craft from offshore racing boats, Atlantic record breakers, patrol boats and large and small powerboats.

There is something for everyone here, from the owner of the 20-knot cruiser to the offshore racing navigator. The rapidly developing world of fast patrol boats and other commercial craft will also benefit from the essentially practical techniques which have been developed from experience. In writing the book I have assumed the reader will have a basic knowledge of navigation – the sort of navigation taught to beginners – including understanding courses, bearings, dead reckoning, etc. The book elaborates on these basic techniques so that they can be used effectively in the sometimes hostile fast boat environment, and covers the use of electronics as well as navigating with the weather.

Navigation is not treated in isolation since it is, in effect, governed by the environment. Fast boats can create a tough environment, which the design of the boat and the navigation equipment can help to alleviate. The human element is an important factor in this type of navigation; merely understanding the techniques will not necessarily prepare you for the conditions in which you have to work. This book will guide you in the right direction; from there on it is practical experience which will complete the lesson.

Although basic techniques for fast boat navigation are explained, the future lies in electronics. At present the general philosophy is that electronics are merely an aid to navigation. In the fast boat environment electronics can transform navigation from intelligent guesswork into positive and accurate information. This change in the approach requires a change in the way electronics are used; a positive approach will ensure that the information from the equipment is correct and can be trusted – or if it can't, that you are aware of the fact. The main change needs to come in the teaching of fast boat navigation because this sets the pattern for use. It needs to recognise the change and concentrate on the intelligent use of electronics, and the back-up systems which are available if the equipment should let you down. Fast boats are in the vanguard of electronic navigation because they are the craft in which traditional techniques are found to be most inadequate. In many areas of electronic navigation the approach is casual because users are taught that they must never rely fully on electronics. In fast boat navigation nothing must be casual; this book shows how electronics can move from being simply an 'aid' to become the primary system of navigation.

1 The high speed environment

Conventional navigation techniques demand two essential ingredients, time and space. You need time to take bearings or gather information to establish your position, and space to lay out the chart and work on it. In this way the raw information is translated into a position on the chart from which you can decide on future action. In fast boats, both time and space can be in short supply; this makes navigation difficult if you try to follow the conventional methods. However, there are techniques for fast boat navigation which make the best use of the time and space available and which will help you cope with the difficulties of the situation.

The whole navigation environment in fast boats is not really conducive to efficient navigation so let's start by exploring it so that we know what we are up against.

TIME

The time factor in navigation is directly related to the speed. At 10 knots, if it takes you a minute to process and plot the navigation information to obtain a position, you will have covered 300 yards – a distance in which nothing dramatic is likely to happen provided you have everything well under control. Compare that to the half mile covered in the same time if you are travelling at 30 knots, and the much greater distances involved if you are travelling at really high speeds. You could easily be a mile away from a fix by the time you have plotted it on the chart, so that it rapidly becomes history, making it more difficult to plan future action. These distances and times are based on being able to use the conventional techniques, but other factors such as vibration and pounding can make them much more difficult to apply in a fast boat so that in fact the time taken to plot a fix could be doubled.

On slow boats, then, you have the luxury of time as far as navigation is concerned, but as speed rises, the time factor becomes more critical. One simple solution is to stop the boat, fix the position and then take off again. In this way you will know where you are at that moment, but it is hardly a satisfying method of navigation. It does, however, have its merits in certain situations particularly if you become uncertain of your position. Then it can be very prudent to stop and work things out.

The other solution is to speed up the navigation process. This will be one of the main approaches in this book. Mental and visual methods of fixing the position can give adequate accuracy for many purposes and give virtually instantaneous fixes. Modern electronic techniques can also give an immediate real-time tactical plot of the situation, and this is the way ahead for fast boat navigation. By using electronic equipment you can bypass the paper chart and so immediately improve the timescale in processing navigation information.

Good preparation is another means of coping with the time factor. By working out as much of the navigation as possible beforehand, you can reduce the time required for the task during the voyage.

You will probably use a combination of all these techniques, depending on the particular situation you find yourself in. However, the important thing is to appreciate the time factor and be aware of the pressures it can put on you, particularly when operating within narrow margins of error.

SPACE

The leisurely activity at the chart table may be a feature of traditional navigation, but in a fast boat moving about can be very difficult, and it is possible that you will be confined to a seat or control position. Space may be limited, and even if you can spread out a chart, the possibility of using it with conventional instruments is remote, given the movement of a fast boat and the need to keep at least one hand free to hold on with to avoid being thrown around the boat.

Like time, space is a luxury on a fast boat. Certainly you will want to find space to lay out a chart, but this will be for reference rather than for plotting, and this is where the techniques of mental and visual navigation and preparation come in. Within the limits of current navigation technology, the paper chart is still an essential item and it is wise to plan space where it can be available for reference. This itself reduces the space requirement because the chart can be folded.

When planning space on board the optimum solution is to have separate control and navigation areas, but this in turn demands a two-man crew to operate the systems. Certainly on smaller craft the trend is towards one-man operation, which can lead to a battle of priorities at the helm with navigation, monitoring and control requirements all having to be allocated priorities. These will be different for different craft, navigation areas and operations, and only the helmsman can really decide in each particular circumstance, but the use of limited space available at the helm has to be considered carefully. (This is looked at in more detail in Chapter 7 on wheelhouse layout.)

Methods of operating within a confined space and with conflicting demands on that space are similar in many respects to those where time is the factor causing pressure. Electronics can help a great deal but much development work is still required to optimise electronic equipment for the fast boat environment, particularly with regard to the amount of space they require for use.

MOTIVATION

This may seem to be a strange factor in fast boat navigation. You are in a fast boat so your motivation is clear: you want to go fast. However, consider the offshore racer, the fast patrol boat operator and the pleasure cruiser and it's easy to see how the motivation and thus the techniques required are different.

The offshore racer is operating over a prescribed course. Preparation features largely in the navigation plan because the navigator knows exactly where he has to go and, to a certain extent, the speeds at which he will be operating. Because of the prescribed course, it is relatively easy to work out all the options. Against this clear cut objective is the fact that the speeds will be very high, probably the highest achieved on the open sea, visibility may be restricted through spray or the rapid movement of the boat and the discomfort can be intense. Particular attention needs to be paid to the layout arrangements to try to optimise the environment because only then will the crew be motivated to excel, to fight the discomfort created by the environment, and to win.

The pleasure boat operator, on the other hand, will put comfort high on his list, which can mean a more relaxed attitude to driving and navigating. Here safety can be a paramount factor particularly if the family is on board, but this leisurely pace designed to produce a relaxed ride may be interspersed with bursts at higher speeds when the driver wants to push the boat closer to the limits, to stretch both himself and the craft. However, there is no pressure or motivation to maintain the pace beyond reason, as there can be in the racing environment, and any signs of overstepping the mark either in the driving or the navigation can be quickly counteracted by a reduction in speed – the only possible problem being loss of pride.

The fast patrol boat operator, however, may have to cope with aspects of both situations. In a chase, racing requirements will come to the fore and the competitive urge will take over. However, there may be occasions when the highest possible speed has to be maintained without the benefit of competition. This is probably the hardest situation in which to find motivation and demands great attention to both driving and navigation. The results, of course, will be subjective because there is very little to measure them against.

On the other hand a patrol boat may be simply on passage or on patrol where speed is not critical but comfort is. A comfortable environment can help to maintain motivation and concentration during long hours of patrol and can be just as important a feature of the design as the hull and machinery.

The motivational aspect of fast boats is difficult, if not impossible, to quantify and so is usually dismissed as irrelevant. The motivation to do one's job may be easier to define, but this tends to be concentrated within the individual. Of course the offshore racer is motivated, otherwise why is he out there – but could he be better motivated if life were made more comfortable, if the discomfort levels were reduced and he could concentrate on the job in hand? I think the answer is a resounding yes, and this aspect of fast boat navigation will need to receive increasing attention if it is to keep pace with the speed potential of modern boats.

It pays to analyse the motivation factor carefully. In all but calm seas it will be the one which determines how fast or for how long the boat can be pushed. It can compensate for bad or inadequate design to a degree, but ideally motivation and design should go hand in hand. This will greatly enhance the potential and the pleasure of the boat. It is in the navigation and control areas that improvements can be made which will have a major impact.

THE MOVEMENT OF THE BOAT

The most debilitating aspect of fast boats is the pounding experienced in waves. This can produce vertical accelerations with transitory values up to $10g$ – some say it can be higher. In offshore racing a value of $15g$ is generally accepted as the design standard for equipment to survive, though this level of pounding will only be experienced when such boats are being pushed very hard. In fast sports boats, patrol boats and similar types of craft, on the other hand, the limit will probably be in the order of $5g$.

The movement of the boat caused by its interaction with waves would be less distressing if it was regular and could be anticipated. One of the major difficulties is the erratic nature of the movement reflecting the constant variations in the waves. This means that movements can occur without warning and there is a need to be constantly alert in order to react against them and remain secure in the boat.

This constant movement takes it toll both mentally and physically. Mentally, there is little chance for relaxation; you quickly become tired and your ability to concentrate is considerably reduced. In severe conditions such as racing your mental ability could probably fall by as much as 50 per cent, a serious reduction which must be taken into account in your planning and actions.

Physically, bracing yourself against the constant movement can be very tiring, and the motion can also make it difficult to perform various functions. Your head and arms will appear to weigh much more than normal because of the g-forces during pounding, and it may not always be possible to make them perform the actions you want.

The pounding and constant movement make life difficult in the fast boat environment, but by careful design and planning a lot can be done to reduce the effect. We will look at this in detail later because it has a considerable bearing on the way you navigate and operate the boat.

VISIBILITY

It sounds obvious to say that you need to be able to see where you are going in a fast boat, but the question of visibility is much more critical in this environment where things tend to happen quickly. There are two aspects to the problem of visibility: the longer range visibility necessary to see the land, navigation marks and other vessels, and the shorter range visibility necessary to read the approaching waves.

The former requires a good all-round view, something which often seems to be sadly lacking on fast boats. Visibility astern can sometimes be zero. It is a misplaced arrogance to suppose that you are the fastest boat on the water and nothing can overtake you. The view ahead and to the side can often be obstructed by wide window frames, and it's easy to get a nasty surprise when other boats or fishing marks suddenly appear quite close the first time you spot them.

Things do happen quickly on a fast boat and it is not always easy to appreciate your speed when in an enclosed wheelhouse. Shut in away from the sea you get little noise and spray, two of the main indications of how fast you are travelling in a relative sense. In this situation good visibility is essential, particularly as you cannot always move about the wheelhouse to look round any blind spots.

The short-range visibility needed to read the waves is equally important. The view ahead can be obstructed by the bow or reduced by railings or fender stowages. Since you are interested mainly in the view two or three waves ahead, you tend to look down, so the trim control can be a useful aid to improve your view. In beam seas, or seas on the bow, you still want to be able to read the waves, so the view at this angle is just as crucial. The view astern is not so important unless you are forced to slow down thus allowing the waves to overtake you; then the view astern can become critical.

There is no doubt, from an operational point of view, that an open steering position is best, but it causes problems keeping things dry and can put extra pressure on the crew through buffeting by the wind. If your motivation for fast boating is pleasure, then there can be an added bonus with the open steering position in terms of wind and sun – in pleasure boating you have the luxury of deciding what weather you will cruise in most of the time.

Darkness brings a different set of visibility problems. It may be difficult if not impossible to read the waves and you will be navigating with lights rather than marks. Bright lights on instrumentation in the wheelhouse and navigation lights shining on the foredeck or rails can cause problems seeing the outside world. Finally, reflections of lights on the windscreen can create a confusing picture since you tend to focus on the reflection on the screen rather than on what lies beyond.

Apart from the difficulty of reading the waves, most of the other night-time problems, once appreciated, can be corrected through improved design or helped by the use of electronics. It's all a question of priorities in the original design concept of the boat, an aspect dealt with in more detail in Chapter 7 on wheelhouse design.

WATER, SPRAY AND WEATHER

Spray is the inevitable result of a boat travelling fast on the water. If you move fast enough you will leave the spray behind, but on many boats spray can be a major problem, particularly when the wind is on the bow or the beam. In these circumstances it picks up the spray and tends to curl it over the driving position which does little for good visibility or comfort.

With an open steering position, the spray makes you wet and impedes concentration. With a closed steering position salt water spray on the screen will smear and reduce visibility, particularly if the spray is intermittent. On a sunny day when the spray dries out quickly, keeping the screen clear can be difficult.

The problem with spray is that there is little to be done about it short of altering your course or your speed. Windscreen wipers and washers help but are rarely the complete answer. Rain can be just as much of a problem. Of course it doesn't smear, but it can reduce visibility and make navigation more difficult. Moreover, it is the one thing that radar does not cope well with.

The main problem with mist and fog is that they reduce the time available in which navigation marks or other craft might be sighted. This increases the need for concentration. Of course, if you don't like the limited time available in poor visibility, there is a simple remedy available: slow down and give yourself more time. Radar is a tremendous boon in mist or fog, but using it effectively in the fast boat environment requires thoughtful installation and design (see Chapter 8).

THE TOTAL ENVIRONMENT

Life is rarely easy in a fast boat. From a navigation point of view, decisions have to be made quickly, while you are in an environment which is not conducive to cohesive thought. Part of the difficulty stems from having a variety of problems occupy your mind, some immediate and some longer term, while at the same time, your concentration is being diverted by the discomfort caused by your surroundings.

Your immediate preoccupation is to read each wave and drive the boat over it. The faster and smaller the boat and the worse the conditions, the greater the need to concentrate on this aspect. In the longer term you also need to relate the course of the boat to land or sea marks or fix its position by electronics.

In between all this, you have to concentrate on the compass and the steering. If you are having to deal with all these things on your own, then you will have a full-time job on your hands if conditions are in any way difficult.

One solution, of course, is to split the workload. One crew member dedicated to navigation leaves the helmsman free to drive the boat, so that each can do a better job. This is the pattern in offshore racing where the work is divided even further, with one crew member on the throttles and trim, one on the steering and the third navigating. In this way, each person can concentrate on a particular job, and this is what enables the boat to be driven to the limits.

On many modern racing boats the crew is reduced to two with the driver also navigating, thus bringing added pressure. It's interesting to note that it is mainly the two-person boats which make navigation mistakes. On a three-person boat, the person on the throttles concentrates on reading the waves, the driver concentrates on the compass or the mark he is steering for, while the navigator scans the horizon for the visual clues to establish position and course. If the driver has to do two jobs, not only does he or she have to switch focus, which is bad for concentration, but in dividing his or her time between two jobs, one will inevitably suffer.

On a racing boat you do not have the option of slowing down to sort out problems – you could lose the race. On most other boats, slowing down buys time and enables you to tackle the problems if the workload becomes too much. Although in theory this option is always available, in practice this is not always the case, because the driver often does not want to lose face by admitting that the task is becoming too much. However, the situation could quickly develop into a greater drama if it is not quickly recognised.

Things like spray, darkness and excessive pounding can add pressure to a situation in which the crew are already stretched to cope. Seasickness and tiredness are other stress factors which can lead to mistakes. In this difficult and changing environment it is important to recognise when the limits are being reached and to try to keep control of the situation.

A great deal can be achieved in the basic design of a fast boat to improve these conditions for navigation – and by navigation I mean the driving of the boat as well as finding the way, since on a fast boat the two go hand in hand. These areas have in the past been neglected by both designers and builders, probably because of lack of experience and knowledge. Not only are there basic problems to be solved such as suitable seating and adequate visibility, but there are also more subtle problems such as being able to operate electronic equipment and having a compass which can be used in a high speed environment. These aspects are dealt with in later chapters of the book.

Given that there is much which can be done to improve the environment, the techniques of navigation themselves are just as important. Because the speed capability of boats has risen only slowly, there has not really been a point at which it could be said that traditional navigation techniques became unsuitable for fast boats. Instead the traditional techniques have been adapted to try to find methods which will work in the often hostile environment.

Electronics have brought a new meaning to high speed navigation, since they can produce answers where traditional techniques fail. However, there are few electronic systems geared to high speeds, so even here there is a need to adapt and modify to make the best of what is available. Nobody likes to place complete reliance on electronic equipment, particularly when they are working in the fast boat environment, so the right solution is a combination of the traditional and the modern.

In the best traditions of navigating, the navigator should use all of the information available. If he is lucky he will have too much so that the surplus can be used to check the basic results; he may have just enough information to cope with the situation – this should be the minimum acceptable level; or he may not have enough, and in this situation, the main need is to recognise the inadequacies so that extra safety margins or cautions can be considered.

The fast boat operator is, perhaps, in the fortunate position of being able to build in extra safety by slowing down, but this is not always a welcome approach. It may be a short-term answer to a particular situation but in the long term there are two effective solutions. One is to improve the navigation environment so that there is every possibility of improving navigation techniques and standards; the other is to explore fully the specialised techniques of high speed navigation so that available information is not wasted.

2 The value of preparation

One of the easiest ways of reducing the navigation workload on fast boats is to transfer some of the work ashore, that is do it before you leave harbour. Aircraft pilots have been doing this for many years, and the problems of increased speed on the water are in many ways similar to those on light aircraft. A great deal of the collision avoidance workload of aircraft has been transferred to the ground and the whole route is planned and plotted before departure. In fast boats, collision avoidance remains firmly in the driver's hands, but a great deal of the navigation can be done before you leave.

Planning and plotting the route before you go can save a great deal of work when you are at sea. It should be the basis of all high speed navigation unless you are prepared to stop or slow down to work things out once you are at sea. In general, the greater the speed, the more preparation you will need to do before you leave harbour. In offshore racing you do as much as is humanly possible before you go because you know that the mental and physical stress will limit your navigation virtually to checking the results of the preparatory work.

The advantage in offshore racing is that you have a prescribed course to follow so you know exactly where you want to go. However, there are invariably numerous options open along the route, either to improve on the sea conditions and their relationship with the boat or to improve navigation. You have to look at all these options and consider plans for both good and poor visibility. You may not need all of this information, but you will not know what you want until you are out there. Out of all the preparatory work on the navigation before a race, you may use only about 20 per cent. But you won't know which 20 per cent you will need until you come to use it.

You will not normally need to go to these lengths in more relaxed fast boating but you cannot afford to ignore the value of preparation if you don't want to be caught out. Poor visibility is probably your biggest enemy – the one which most needs your preparation – so if there is any hint of fog, get your charts out before you go.

CHARTWORK

Preparation work starts with the chart. Here you have the basis of all your navigation; the chart is the interface between the position you determine when you are out at sea, and the land, rocks, shoals, navigation marks, etc. If you think about this concept of an interface it will give you a much better idea of how the chart is used in high speed navigation. It displays the navigation situation (in real-time if you have just put a position on the chart), but it is just as valuable if you are in circumstances where you cannot write but can instead 'imagine' your position on the chart.

We will go into the role of the chart in more detail when we look at eyeball navigation in Chapter 3 and the use of electronics in Chapter 4, but for your preparation work the first step is to draw a line or lines on the chart to represent the course you want to follow. You may want to adjust this line later, but that initial line represents the starting point from which you can plan your route in more detail. You will need this line on the chart whether you are using basic eyeball navigation or electronics for position fixing.

If that line is the route you want to follow, then obviously it should not pass close to or over any dangers. The next stage is to follow along the line, studying the chart carefully to see what lies in the vicinity of the line in terms of dangers. Shallow water, rocks and, of course, land all represent dangers to navigation, and when I am navigating I highlight any of these danger areas which lie close to the planned route so that I remain aware of them.

In racing you only use the chart once, so here a highlighting pen is useful to emphasise the dangerous areas. For routine navigation you won't want to spoil the chart so a soft (4B) pencil is ideal to put a ring around the danger. This gives a strong dark line, particularly if the pencil is not very sharp.

The navigation chart is designed for use under what the publishers would describe as 'normal' conditions, i.e. where it can be studied under reasonable light in calm waters. Some of the printing is very small so that as much detail as possible can be included. Unfortunately some of this detail can be very hard to make out under the conditions found in a fast boat. With your head and eyes moving, sometimes involuntarily in relation to the chart, the detail becomes blurred, and the aim of the highlighting is to modify the chart so that you can still identify the important features on it at high speed.

Having studied the route in relation to the dangers, you may want to modify the course to give a greater margin of safety. We will look at the safety aspect later, but in general you do not want to pass too close to underwater dangers that you can't see.

The next stage is to follow along the route on the chart to find any navigation

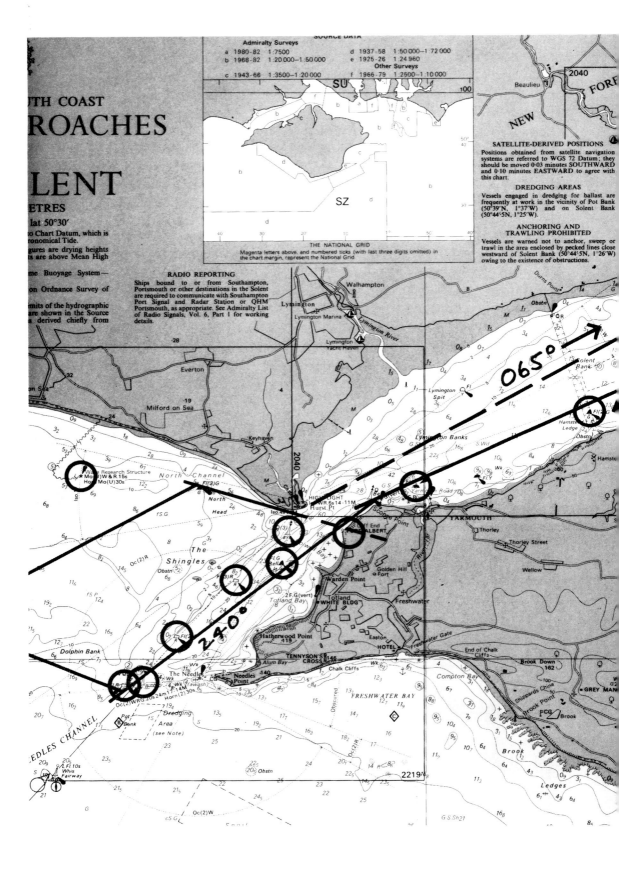

UTH COAST

ROACHES

LENT

ETRES

lat 50°30′

o Chart Datum, which is
ronomical Tide.

gures are drying heights
ts are above Mean High

me Buoyage System—

on Ordnance Survey of

mits of the hydrographic
are shown in the Source
a derived chiefly from

SOURCE DATA

Admiralty Surveys

a	1980-82	1:7500	d	1937-58	1:50 000-1:72 000
b	1968-82	1:20 000-1:50 000	e	1925-26	1:24 960
c	1943-66	1:3500-1:20 000	f	1966-79	1:2500-1:10 000

Other Surveys

THE NATIONAL GRID
Magenta letters above, and numbered ticks (with last three digits omitted) in
the chart margin, represent the National Grid

RADIO REPORTING
Ships bound to or from Southampton,
Portsmouth or other destinations in the Solent
are required to communicate with Southampton
Port Signal and Radar Station or QHM
Portsmouth, as appropriate. See Admiralty List
of Radio Signals, Vol. 6, Part 1 for working
details.

SATELLITE-DERIVED POSITIONS
Positions obtained from satellite navigation
systems are referred to WGS 72 Datum; they
should be moved 0·03 minutes SOUTHWARD
and 0·10 minutes EASTWARD to agree with
this chart.

DREDGING AREAS
Vessels engaged in dredging for ballast are
frequently at work in the vicinity of Pot Bank
(50°39′N, 1°37′W) and on Solent Bank
(50°44′·5N, 1°25′W).

ANCHORING AND
TRAWLING PROHIBITED
Vessels are warned not to anchor, sweep or
trawl in the area enclosed by pecked lines close
westward of Solent Bank (50°44′·5N, 1·26′W)
owing to the existence of obstructions.

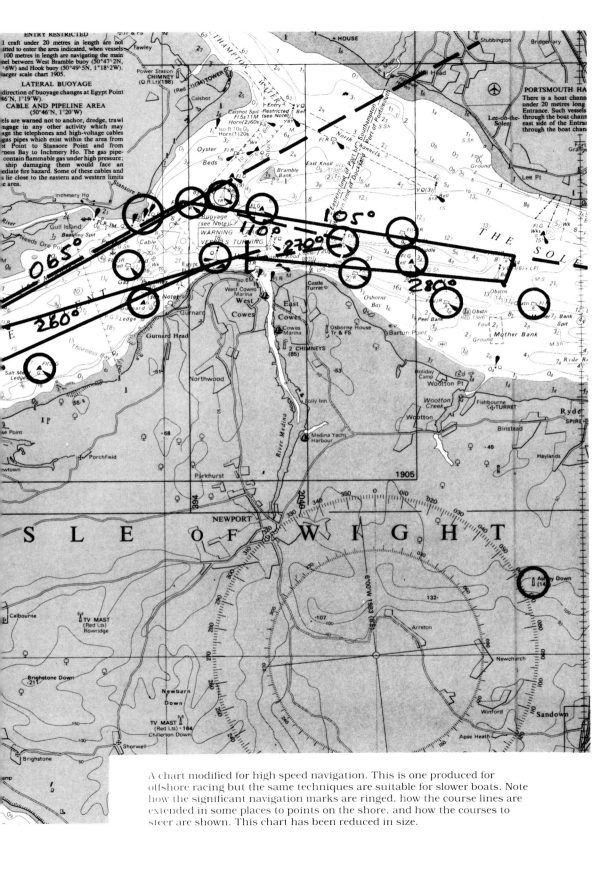

A chart modified for high speed navigation. This is one produced for offshore racing but the same techniques are suitable for slower boats. Note how the significant navigation marks are ringed, how the course lines are extended in some places to points on the shore, and how the courses to steer are shown. This chart has been reduced in size.

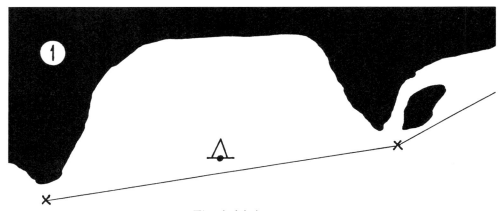

The initial course

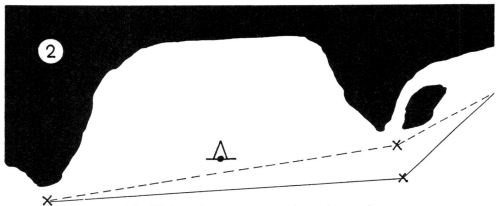

Modifying the course to clear the rock

2nd modification to pass close to the buoy

The stages in setting out the course to get the optimum for eyeball navigation. This is the sequence of operations, but once you become experienced you draw the final line automatically.

marks close to the course. Once again you highlight these because they are important guides. I put a pencil ring round a buoy or mark and, if necessary, a letter to indicate its colour.

Once again you may want to fine tune the route to take you closer to one or more of these marks. Any navigation mark close to your course is very valuable because it is an accurate check on your position. It can pay to put a shallow dog-leg into the route just to pass close to a buoy because sighting it will give a check on progress and give you valuable peace of mind.

Check again that any alterations do not bring you close to any of the dangers you marked previously. Once you are satisfied, this line will be your chosen route and you can measure off the course and distance of each leg.

You will want these courses and distances available at sea, and here you have a choice. You can write the courses and distances on the chart alongside the route line or you can use a separate sheet of paper. In racing I do both because I am always nervous about losing one piece of paper, and the list of courses and distances gives the other crew members an idea of what is going on. Try to use figures at least one inch high; anything smaller may be difficult to read clearly on a bouncing boat.

As far as courses are concerned, the ones you write on the chart should correspond with the compass. With a magnetic compass you will apply the variation and deviation on the course taken off the chart, so that the figure you write down is the *actual* course you steer. This avoids mistakes and the mental arithmetic necessary to apply the corrections. Some electronic compasses have the facility to correct automatically for variation, so if this is the

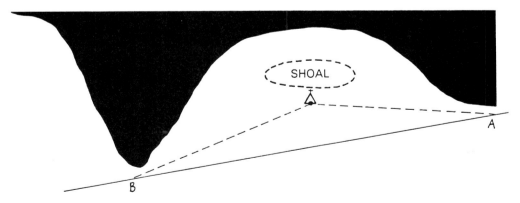

Deviating to find a buoy can reduce the distance you have to travel between marks. On the straight line from A to B you could be a mile or two off course by the time you get to B. Diverting via the buoy reduces the chance of error.

case with yours then obviously it is necessary to apply only the deviation to the course taken off the chart.

TIDES

In a fast boat you can generally ignore tides because the effect is very small compared with the speed at which you are travelling. Certainly when travelling along a coast the tide will have only a minimal effect on your course, although it could make a small difference to your speed. The main circumstances under which you need to consider tides are when they are on the beam and your boat

It's only in strong cross tides that you need be concerned with what the tides are doing. You may be more concerned with the effect of the tide on the sea conditions (see Chapter 12).

speed is under 40 knots. Even then they will only be a real problem on a leg of 20 miles or more, but in poor visibility where you want a more accurate check on your course and where speeds may be slower, adjust your course to compensate for any tide.

Part of your preparation work should of course involve checking the tides. Because you want to have to remember as little as possible it is a good idea to have a board on which you can write the times of the tide. It's not just the tidal flow which you may have to consider, but also the height of tide if you plan to cut any corners in shallow water.

Probably the biggest effect of the tide will be on the sea conditions. Wind against tide, or current for that matter, can knock up a nasty short, steep sea. This can be in dramatic contrast to the same area when wind and tide are acting together with strong tides. For a fast boat, the change in conditions can make a huge difference to your progress, so this is exactly the sort of thing you need to take into account in your preparation.

The chart is a mine of information, but it will not show this type of sea condition, except where the tides are strong and the effects consistent and severe. Most charts will show areas where tide races or rips are likely to be found and in general these are to be avoided in a fast boat. They are usually present off headlands or in narrow channels, but can also be generated around sandbanks, so look out for these areas on the chart when plotting your course. Often the sea area can be affected when the tide changes direction; more information can be found in pilot books. Remember also that when pilot books describe such conditions, they tend to do so in relation to their effect on slow displacement boats rather than fast planing boats. A general rule is to avoid such areas, unless you have local knowledge.

WEATHER

Weather conditions play an important part in any high speed operation, and so an essential part of your preparation should be to study the weather forecasts. The normal marine forecasts give a good idea of the general weather situation, but often are not detailed enough for you to use the weather conditions to best advantage. For instance, the forecast may speak of freshening winds, with little or no clue about the timing of the change.

For a fast boat, timing is all important as far as the weather is concerned because you will often have the ability to overtake the weather change or to run before it. You can dictate where you are in relation to a particular weather pattern – something a slower boat cannot do. Because of your high speed you can often complete a passage before a forecast change comes along. You have

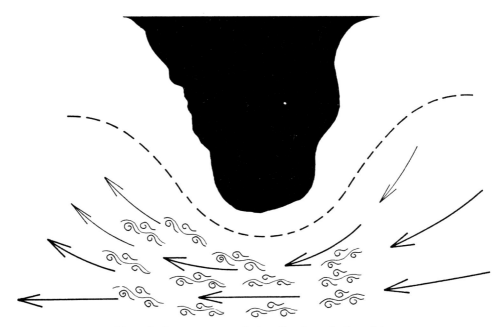

It is sometimes possible to find a course round a headland inside the tidal
race, but you need local knowledge or advice before taking such a course. It
will only be feasible if there are no rocks or shoals off the headland.

the ability to negotiate with the weather, but you can only do this if you have a
more detailed picture of what the weather is doing than is generally available
from normal marine forecasts.

Finding a source of good forecasts can be difficult, but principally what you
need are weather maps which show in detail where the fronts which herald
changes are located and the speed at which they are moving. If you can't get
these charts then the next best thing is to discuss the weather with a
forecaster. In most areas the telephone directory will provide the information
you need to be able to contact a forecaster at the local weather information
centre; if not, the harbour master or marina control will be able to help.

When you have the forecast, relate the expected weather conditions to your
proposed route. Remember that winds and sea conditions off headlands will
generally be stronger than in bays. With offshore winds, the sea area adjacent
to the land will be sheltered, but with onshore winds the seas will be much
rougher and where there are sheer cliffs there could be waves reflected off the
cliffs causing a confused wave pattern. At the end of the day it is not the wind
that counts, but its effect on the sea. The tides also have their part to play – it is
really only experience which will enable you to make a wise judgement.

PREPARATION FOR NIGHT NAVIGATION

At night the whole navigation environment changes. It is difficult to see the waves, and other craft have to be recognised by lights rather than as good solid objects, all of which serves to make life more troublesome. To this you have to add the difficulties of working in a darkened wheelhouse where the chart may not be easily visible and where you have to work the controls by touch as much as by sight.

You will not travel as quickly at night as in daytime, so at least you have time on your side, but preparatory work is just as important. Navigating in relation to flashing lights is difficult at high speed, but at least if you write down the characteristics of the lights (either on the chart in readable letters or on a separate card) then you will be able to identify them more readily when you approach them. Steering compass courses can also be more important at night since you have less in the way of visual heading references, so always make sure you have these courses at hand, even in familiar waters.

ALTERNATIVES AND SAFETY MARGINS

In your planning it pays to err on the side of safety. Unpredicted changes can and do occur at sea and you want a margin of safety to give you a chance to sort things out if you make mistakes or if problems occur. When planning the route on the chart you should allow a margin from such dangers as sandbanks and rocks in case the course you make good does not match up to the course you put on the chart. If the danger is marked with a buoy or beacon, however, you can reduce your safety margin because you should see the mark before you get into trouble with the shallow water. Indeed in this case you don't really want to allow a margin at all, otherwise you could miss the mark altogether and only find the shallow water when you touch bottom.

If you are working with electronic position fixing then your margins could be smaller because you have a more precise indication of your position, but watch out for the equipment giving information which is less than accurate. It is always very precise in appearance, but it may not be as accurate as it seems (see Chapter 4). Otherwise this matter of safety margins is a delicate balance. On the one hand you don't want to get too close to the danger you are trying to avoid, and on the other hand you don't want to go so far out to sea that you might miss future marks which guide you along your course. It is a matter of careful and balanced judgement and one which you can assess much better in the calm of a marina berth than when bouncing around at sea.

The same principles apply when looking at alternative courses along the route. These could take advantage of changes in the wind and sea conditions, could deviate to find shelter in a strengthening wind or could give a safer route in the event of fog. Other options to consider are which ports could be alternatives to your destination if you run into trouble, for example if you have engine problems. Some ports may only be accessible at certain states of tide, or these same ports might only have berths which dry out at low water which is not welcome news for most fast boats. Time spent on the chart looking at all the possibilities is never wasted; even if you do not use the information you have worked out, it will add to your fund of experience which is really what high speed navigation is all about.

THE VALUE OF PREPARATION

All this seems a great deal of effort to go to before you go off to sea and on the first occasion you make such preparations they will take some time. Much of the work will not be used when you get out to sea, and you will probably start to think that it has all been a waste of time. Moreover, much that you have gleaned from studying the chart will remain in your mind, adding to the wealth of experience which will one day turn you into an expert.

It is easy to assume that you don't need to write everything down when you are doing the preparation work; you think you will easily remember it when the time comes out at sea. This is a false assumption. The notion of a fast boat driven hard will soon drive most other thoughts out of your mind as well, except those of coping with this exhilarating and sometimes hostile environment. A conventional chart can change into a meaningless blur under these conditions, so the need to tailor the chart information to the requirements of high speed navigation should be obvious. You can use the conventional parallel rules and dividers for plotting in harbour but they will not be of much use out at sea.

In developing the chart by highlighting specific features of interest you are converting it into one which can be used, at least visually, in the high speed environment. You will develop your own shorthand to put information on the chart in a meaningful way so that you will get what you want from it. One day chart publishers may produce special charts to meet the requirements of fast boats, but long before that time the electronic chart will probably have taken over.

Even if you are navigating by electronics already you should still carry out this chart preparation work. First, the equipment may break down and you will be forced to resort to basic navigation techniques. Secondly, unless your position-fixing by electronics is linked up to an electronic chart, the information presented by the equipment will only be of real value if you can relate it to the chart.

With experience you will learn a lot of short cuts in your preparation work. Going for a quick trip across the bay on a route you know well does not require the same detailed preparation as a long trip along the coast. You will know the buoys and recognise the land features so that you can be more relaxed about the preparation, but even in these familiar surroundings it pays to have the chart available with the courses marked on it. You may turn round a buoy and not be able immediately to pick up the next mark that you want to steer to. In this situation it is very reassuring to have a course to follow until you get your bearings.

Electronic navigation will give you most of the answers you are looking for in order to proceed safely. For instance, it can give you the course and distance to the next point you are heading for at the touch of a button. However, it will only produce this information if it has been programmed to do so, and the programming of the equipment has to be part of your preparation work.

However you navigate, you should not go to sea casually on a fast boat. The rapidly changing navigation environment could catch up with you very quickly if you haven't done your preparation; you will then have to stop or slow down to get your bearings. This is not a tidy way to navigate and you could find yourself in greater difficulties if the conditions change. Once you have the knack the preparation doesn't take long and experience will soon tell you what is necessary – but don't rely on your memory too much. A checklist is an excellent idea and will prevent you from going to sea unprepared.

3   Eyeball navigation

'Eyeball navigation' is really what it says, using your eyes to navigate. It means coming down to basics, using a compass and a watch, supplemented perhaps by a log and an echo sounder if these can be made to work in a fast boat. In this environment you can do little navigation work with your hands; you can't use a hand bearing compass to fix the position, so all you are left with is the information from your preparation work and what you can see, hence the phrase 'eyeball navigation'. Now you will begin to appreciate how important the preparation work is, because without it what you see may not have much meaning.

Traditional navigation techniques consist of measuring various parameters and translating them into a position on the chart. We have already established how difficult it is to use the chart in the fast boat environment; it is equally difficult to measure distances in order to establish position. Moreover, by using your eyes you can only make approximate measurements. Distances and bearings can be judged with a limited accuracy which can be of help, but there are also a number of other clues to your position out at sea. Although none of these clues may give you a high level of accuracy, when you add them all together you will start to get a fairly good picture of where you are and, more importantly, where you are going.

In some ways eyeball navigation embodies many of the techniques employed in pilotage which is generally used in the confines of ports and harbours or narrow channels. In these areas you have plenty of well defined indicators to your position – buoys, beacons, leading lights, etc. Out at sea you will still have some of these positive indicators but to supplement them you need to use the more subtle clues which are available. With eyeball navigation you do not necessarily need to know your position in absolute terms, but in terms relative to your route or to dangers. For instance, if you see a ferry operating on a known route this can give you an indication of your position, or if you can see the surf breaking on shallow water, then you know where you are in relation to that shoal even though you may not be able to pinpoint your precise position on the chart. In this sort of navigation, relative accuracy can be just as important as absolute accuracy.

WAYPOINT NAVIGATION

This is an appropriate point at which to introduce waypoint navigation. It has achieved popularity with the introduction of electronics, but it is an equally valid technique with eyeball navigation and will help to give you a better picture of what is going on. Because you cannot write on the chart as you are going along, you have to visualise your situation, plotting in an abstract way so that you have your position fixed mentally if not physically. I find that waypoint navigation can help with this visualisation.

Using waypoint navigation your route is pinpointed by a series of waypoints; these are the points on the route where you alter course. The routes joining these waypoints are straight lines which you will have established in your preparation session. With electronic navigation the waypoint is delineated by latitude and longitude because that is the language the navigation computer understands. With eyeball navigation, on the other hand, the waypoint is simply the point you have marked on the chart. Latitude and longitude do not have much meaning in eyeball navigation, but bearings and distances do.

When you leave one waypoint and head for the next, you want to stay on the straight line joining these two points. Follow that line and you must arrive at the next waypoint, but you also need to take into account the distance you need to travel along the line otherwise you will not know when you have arrived at the waypoint. Electronics can provide this information at the press of a button, giving you an absolute position in terms of latitude and longitude and a relative position in terms of the bearing and distance to the next waypoint.

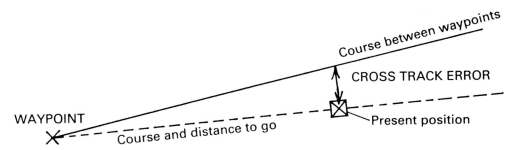

The cross track error shows the distance off course, and this, together with the course and distance to go, shows where you are in relation to the waypoint.

These are valuable pieces of information. If you know the bearing, you know the course to steer to get to the waypoint. Hopefully the bearing will correspond with your original course which means that you are still on the line you drew on the chart. However, the chances are that the wind, tide and helmsman's bias will all combine to throw you off course. It is difficult to judge by a small change in the bearing how far you are off course, so a third parameter is introduced: the cross track error.

As a fast boat navigator, cross track error is one of the most valuable pieces of information you can have. If you are off course to one side or the other you may be closer to dangers that you planned to pass with a certain clearance. Also it means that you won't reach the next waypoint if you maintain your present course, so sooner or later you must do something about it. Whatever type of navigation you are using, cross track error is the best information you can have to help you visualise where you are in relation to where you want to be. (It's also worth remembering that if you know where you are in relation to where you want to be, then you know where you are!)

One of the major benefits of electronics is that they will give you the cross track error on demand. With eyeball navigation you will have to work harder to obtain the information because you will probably not know your position accurately. However, if you use the clues relating to your position which are available to you in an intelligent way, you should be able to get some idea at least of what the cross track error is.

With waypoint navigation, then, there are three parameters which interest you: the bearing and distance to the next waypoint and the cross track error. If you have two of these it is possible to work out the third, but the important thing is that these parameters help you to visualise what is happening in relation to the waypoint ahead. With eyeball navigation, if you relate the clues that you get from various sources to one or more of these parameters then they will start to make sense and relate to the waypoint itself.

COURSES AND DISTANCES

Courses and distance to the next waypoint is the basis of waypoint navigation; this is the information you mark on the chart in your preparation work. The direct line may not be the actual course you steer because you may have to make adjustments for tide effects. The wind can also have an effect if it is on the beam and fast boats with a high superstructure can make leeway just like a sail boat. This leeway effect, however, is likely to be small overall, and unless you are aware of a particular leeway effect on your boat there is little need to make allowances for it.

A more important factor is the helmsman's bias – I'm sure this is one of the main reasons why navigators still find themselves not arriving at a waypoint, no matter how careful they are with their navigation. In my experience most helmsmen bias their steering to one side or the other without realising they are doing so. In many cases it will only be a couple of degrees or so, but it can be up to ten degrees and that can have a serious effect on the course made good. The worst cases are likely to occur when the wind and sea are on the bow; in these conditions there is a general tendency to steer off the wind because it gives a more comfortable ride.

There are no hard and fast rules about helmsman's bias. The only way to find out if it is present is to watch the course being steered and come to your own conclusions. Few helmsmen will admit to biasing the steering, yet most seem to do so. The problem really starts when you yourself are on the wheel. Will you admit to a bias, or will you get someone to watch your steering?

You can't plan for steering bias before you go to sea because you don't know what to allow for. The only thing to do is to watch and correct as you go along, or better still, steer the boat by autopilot. However, even an autopilot can have a bias if it is of the deadband type. The deadband is the angle by which the heading can change before the pilot starts to do something about it; typically this can be 2 degrees either side of the mean heading. Instead of following the mean course the autopilot can run along one side of the deadband thereby introducing a bias into the course. Watching the course and knowing your autopilot are the only ways to find out if this is the case. Even with a bias, however, the autopilot will probably be much more accurate than any human.

Apart from visual checks such as transit bearings or the time you pass headlands when available, there are two possibilities for measuring distance. One is to fit a log that works and let that do the measuring. However, logs are notoriously unreliable in fast boats, not because of the log itself but because the water flow over the transducer can be erratic as the boat rises and falls in the water. Some logs measure only speed, so you will have to do mental calculations with your watch to work out the distance.

The other option is to use the engine rpm and have a close idea from trials or experience about the relationship between rpm and speed. You will realise that you are unlikely to get an accurate measure of distance from either of these sources, so naturally you will use this figure with caution. The faster you travel, the greater the inaccuracy, in general.

To help with your mental plotting of the distance on the chart, it helps if you make a mark every 5 miles or so along the track. This will enable you to get a better idea of where you are in relation to features on the chart, and where you pass close to a feature or navigation mark you can give a precise distance.

Whilst we are on the subject of distances, it can also be helpful to measure off and mark down the distance you expect to pass off notable features which are shown on the chart. This will help you in your mental plotting.

POSITION FIXING

With eyeball navigation there is only one way you can fix your position with any degree of accuracy and that is to pass close to a buoy or other navigation mark. The buoy is in a known position so it means that you are as well. When you do this, remember that buoys are laid to mark a danger of some sort, so don't get close to the danger while trying to get close to a buoy. In most cases you won't have a problem, because buoys tend to be laid to mark the deep water required for ships so there is usually plenty of margin for small boats inside the buoy.

Take more care with beacons. These marks are often built on the danger itself, usually a rock, so you need to give them a reasonable margin. Whether it is a buoy or a beacon, the chart will show you what the margins are so you can judge your position accordingly.

Because they are so useful for fixing your position accurately, it is often a good idea to set your course from buoy to buoy even though it may mean a slight deviation from the direct route. The more updates you can get on your position, the more relaxed you can be and the less chance there is of course deviations taking you away from the chosen route. You don't always have to

Passing a buoy gives an accurate fix in eyeball navigation and it can be worth diverting from the straight line course to obtain such a fix.

pass close to the buoy to get a good check, but you must pass close enough to make sure you see the buoy allowing a margin for being off course. On a fast boat you can't bank on seeing a buoy more than about a mile away, particularly if there is a sea running, so on a short leg you could arrange to pass ½ mile off and still expect to see it, whilst on a longer leg you would be better off heading straight for the buoy. Picking up a buoy in this way can give you a good check on your cross track error.

POSITION LINES

The standard way of fixing positions at sea is by position lines. A position line is a line on a chart somewhere along which the boat lies. One position line will not fix your position, but it will narrow down the sea area in which your boat can be. With two position lines you have a precise fix where the two lines cross, assuming always that the position lines are accurate. If the position line is less accurate, then you have a sector fanning out from where the position line starts, and the boat should lie inside this sector. This is still valuable information and you could narrow down your possible position by having two sectors intersect so that the boat lies somewhere in the diamond formed by the intersection.

Now you are unlikely to be able to plot any position lines on the chart on a fast boat so you have to develop the technique of mental plotting, looking and estimating where the lines or intersections are on the chart. If there are some obvious position lines which you expect to use – perhaps a chimney and a church spire in line – then you can mark these on the chart in dotted lines before you go, or it could be the case that they are already on the chart if they are fairly important.

In the traditional form of navigation the position lines are established by taking bearings with a hand bearing compass. This technique won't be possible unless you stop the boat, but there are many other position lines available to you simply by looking. This is where the detective work starts: each line on its own may seem rather vague, but add all the clues together and you can work out fairly accurately where you are.

Generally position lines come in two forms: those parallel or nearly parallel to your course which can give you a check on the direction you are steering and the vital cross track error, and those which cross your route at or nearly at a right angle which give a check on the distance you have travelled. Try not to ignore any of them because they will all contribute to improving the accuracy of your estimate of where you are and where you are going.

The land can be a rich source of navigation information. A useful part of your preparation would be to ring on the chart all conspicous features such as chimneys, church spires, lighthouses, tall buildings and headlands. When you are travelling along a coastline the waypoints where you alter course will generally be off the headlands, but the other features will give you an indication of your progress along the coastline. When the feature is on the beam you have an approximate bearing which gives you a fix of sorts where the bearing intersects with the course line. This will not indicate the vital cross track error which is what you really want to know, but features like these are not to be ignored.

There will be times when features on the land will come in line and then you have an accurate visual bearing without the help of a compass. These transit bearings are always useful because of their accuracy and if you find any close to the course that you will be following, then they are doubly useful because they can give an indication of the cross track error.

Even a single conspicuous feature ahead is valuable, particularly if your waypoint is located at a buoy – as it usually is when racing. The conspicuous feature may show up ten miles or more away, but the buoy may be only a mile off or less. If there is land shown behind the buoy on the chart, then extend the course line to the land and look for any conspicuous features in the vicinity. They may not be directly on the line, but when you pick up the feature you can

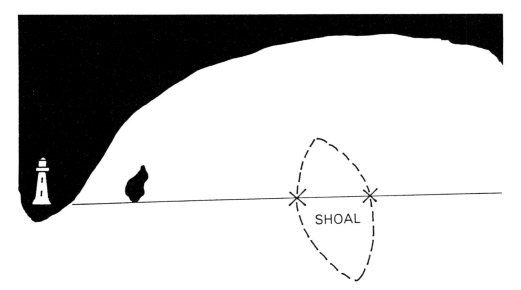

There are possibilities for transits using soundings, islands and shoals. With a lighthouse or similar structure ahead and the echo sounder showing the edge of the shoal you have a useful check on position. Similarly, the edge of the island in line with the lighthouse gives you a good position line.

put it to one side or the other of the boat's head and, combined with checking the course line, this is a sure way of finding the buoy and checking your cross track error at the same time.

When your waypoint lies off a headland then the headland itself will be a good guide. Unless you are in poor visibility the headland will show up in good time to adjust your course to pass the required distance off. Heading across a bay you can often pick up one headland before you loose the last, and looking astern to see where you have come from is just as valid as checking the course ahead. This can also provide a useful check on your cross track error.

Now let's look at some of the more subtle ways of establishing position lines. Shipping can often give you a clue because it tends to follow prescribed routes, particularly where there are routing systems marked on the chart. The introduction of these one-way shipping routes can be a great help because if you pick up shipping heading in a certain direction you can identify the lane it is operating in. These lanes are usually only a few miles wide so it narrows down the options of where you can be.

Ferries tend to operate on much more precise routes so if you sight a ferry it can give you quite an accurate position line. Of course you have to known the ferry and its route and make sure that there isn't any ambiguity, but ferries can be one of the many clues which help to confirm your position.

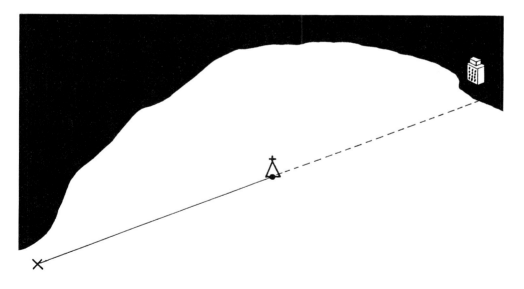

A conspicuous point on the shore can give a useful pointer to finding a buoy. Even if it does not lie directly on the extended line from the buoy it can give you a good idea of where to steer.

Tide rips and races, changes in the colour of the water and similar indications can all help too. I have seen an experienced pilot look over the side of a ship in thick fog and know where he was simply by the swirl in the water over a relatively shallow patch. This requires years of experience, but many of the more obvious features of the sea are marked on the chart and you can use these to help. You may not want to get mixed up in the broken water of tide races and rips, but there are often clear cut edges to the broken water which can be a good guide to where you are.

The same applies with shallow water and here you can often see the sea or swell breaking on the shoal which will indicate its presence. If you have set your course to avoid the shoal, then this breaking sea will be a clear guide, provided of course that you don't see it close to your course line. Changes in water colour will tend to occur off river mouths or when passing from shallow to deep water, or vice versa when the sea is very clear. In open water you can find a change when you enter the Gulf Stream from the colder waters of the Labrador current. This is not a reliable guide but every clue helps.

SOUNDINGS

The changes in the sea bed can often be indicated on the surface of the water when it is shallow, but you can use the sea bed to much greater advantage when you have a working echo sounder. It is doubtful whether you will get an echo sounder to work at speeds over 40 knots. The operating maximum could be much less, so use an echo sounder with caution, but if it will work then it can give valuable information.

By knowing the water depth you have something in the way of a position line. Some depth information is better than others, a sea bed which has considerable variations in depth being much more useful than one with uniform depth. It is the change in depth shown on the echo sounder which can narrow down your position quite accurately. A change in the depth running across the course line will give you a good idea of your progress along the route whilst one running parallel will help you to determine the cross track error. A study of the chart can often show up useful sea bed features which can help your navigation and it may be a good idea to vary the course slightly so that you can take advantage of these features.

Even just isolated soundings can be useful. If you get a depth reading of 20 feet you know you can't be in the areas on the chart showing 50 feet, so it can help to narrow down your position. Likewise, when approaching a headland the change in depth could give you an indication of the distance off when the depths start to shoal as you close the land.

Don't take depth information too literally. The echo sounder itself may not be too accurate unless you have taken the trouble to calibrate it, whilst the effects of tide will also vary the depth. You can, of course, correct for the height of the tide, but don't forget the depth of sea bed itself could have changed from that shown on the chart since it was drawn up, particularly in areas with a sandy bottom. Like much of the information you gather with high speed navigation, soundings are another clue which can help to confirm a position or make you wary about where you are. One thing, however: if the soundings start to shoal where you don't expect them to, this should set the alarm bells ringing and make you navigate with caution until your position becomes clearer.

JUDGING DISTANCES

There is one way of fixing your position which may lack sufficient accuracy to satisfy navigation purists but which I find extremely valuable when navigating fast boats. The method is simple; you simply judge your distance off a headland or a navigation mark, combine this with an estimate of the bearing, and you have an indication of where you are. It requires a little experience to be able to judge the distances reasonably accurately, but it is not too difficult if you take the trouble to practise estimating when you are at sea.

The value of this method is that it can give you a fix of sorts when there is not much else available. For instance, there may be rocks or shallow water extending off a headland so that you have to pass some distance off. With eyeball navigation, there is not much to guide you in this except perhaps soundings, so why not rely on your judgement? You should be able to tell the difference between being half a mile and a mile off, which will be adequate for most practical purposes, and I find that I tend to err on the side of safety and pass further off just to be sure.

You can use the same sort of technique when you are approaching the headland, judging the angle of the headland on the bow as you approach and fine tuning it as you get closer. You can follow the same procedure with a buoy, judging your distance off to get some idea of your cross track error. Operating in buoyed channels and in the confines of a harbour you will use your judgement of distance to track your position; such methods are equally valid at sea, particularly if you can combine them with one of the other position lines we have already looked at. Your judgement of distance is one more clue in the position puzzle – and it can be a very valuable one when you have little else available.

LANDFALLS

Navigating along a coastline you will normally have plenty of clues as to your position, certainly enough in most cases to be reasonably happy about where you are. However, your eyeball navigation is put to a more severe test when you go out of sight of land, perhaps crossing a large bay or making an open sea crossing. You will set your course to the best of your ability, allowing for outside influences on the boat and the helmsman's bias, but making that landfall at the end of the passage can still be a nervous time.

To take some of the guesswork out of the situation there are techniques that will give you a more positive landfall. These involve selecting your landfall point with great care and not necessarily heading for the most obvious point. The idea is to head for a spot where you can still make a safe landfall even if there are errors in the course you steer. This technique should not be an excuse to be casual about setting your course, but it will give you some peace of mind if you do get set off course on your way across.

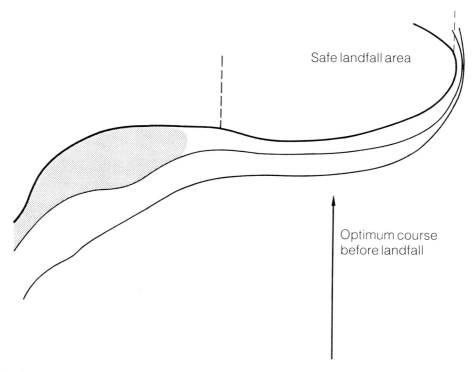

Safe landfall area

Optimum course before landfall

The chart will show areas where you can make a safe landfall in fog. If you aim for the headland you could miss it altogether, but aiming inside the headland allows for steering errors to a certain degree.

If you are heading across a large bay then finding the headland at the other side is important. If you inadvertently head out to seaward of the headland then you could find yourself going past it without realising it if the visibility is not too good. The solution here is to head for a point inside the headland so that any error will still show land up ahead at the end of the crossing. You could be some way inside the headland, but by the time you sight land you can adjust the course to the headland itself; the extra distance added on to the route will be minimal. Check on the chart that there are no serious offlying dangers inside the headland which could cause you embarrassment if the visibility is not good and you find yourself trying to make a landfall on them.

Making a landfall on a stretch of coastline coming in from seaward would seem to be a straightforward exercise – even if you are off course you will eventually make landfall somewhere. That is one way of approaching the problem but it is not very efficient; you will be much better off studying the chart carefully in order to find the optimum place for your landfall. Essentially you are looking for two things. One is a stretch of coastline which you can approach safely without deep bays, and the other is a coastline which has readily identifiable features.

The shape of the coastline is important because you don't really want to head into a deep bay wondering where the land has got to after you have run for the allotted time. However, most ports and harbours are located in bays, so if yours is a deeply indented coastline it's probably best to head for the centre of the bay, which should make sure that at least you end up in the right bay. If the visibility is reasonable you should pick up one or other of the adjacent headlands on the way in, which will give you a reassuring check on your position and enable you to fine tune the approach to your destination.

Identifiable features are needed on the coastline so that you can confirm your landfall as you approach. Headlands, lighthouses, chimneys, towers, factories and conspicuous buildings can all help to identify which part of a coastline you have made your landfall on, but be warned that it is very easy to make what you see fit what you think you ought to see. Try to find a conspicuous feature which is not repeated along the coast so that there will not be any ambiguity.

Some coastlines are featureless and flat and it can be disconcerting making landfall here because everything looks the same. One solution is to introduce a bias into the course so that you know that you will arrive to one side of your destination and there will be no guesswork in deciding which way to turn.

These are some ideas to take the guesswork out of making a landfall. It is not possible to give hard and fast rules because every situation is different – different coastlines, different features, different visibility limits – but the idea should be to reduce the element of chance as far as possible. In a fast boat you can be closing the land fairly rapidly, and ultimately, if you are not happy with what you see, you can always slow down and make the approach at a more leisurely pace.

SECOND-STAGE NAVIGATION

In all this discussion on eyeball navigation we have assumed that when you have plotted and steered the right course you have eventually arrived at your destination. There may be several waypoints along your route and the worry of any navigator is: 'What happens if I don't find the buoy or other mark that I am looking for at the end of each leg of the route?' This is certainly a worry when you are racing offshore because some of the marks require pinpoint navigation, something difficult to guarantee in the racing environment. So, as a good navigator, you will want to keep something up your sleeve in case the mark doesn't turn up where you expect it.

The first thing to recognise, of course, is that you have reached the assumed point and have not found what you are looking for. However, if you wait until that precise moment to try to sort out the problem you have probably left it too late – you will be assuming that you are at the mark and will therefore not know which way to turn to find it when it's not where you expect it to be. In this situation you will almost certainly go past the mark, hoping against hope that it will turn up before you have to admit defeat. From that point you will really be struggling because you are, to all intents and purposes, lost. If you want to have a plan to cope with such a possibility then you have to build this in from the start and not hope to pick up the pieces when things have gone wrong.

If you are trying to find an isolated mark there is no substitute for setting an accurate course at the start. Your compass needs to be compensated and accurate. You need to apply the correction for variation and deviation, perhaps also an allowance for tide, and then you must watch for the helmsman's bias. If you get all these things right then you should arrive at the mark spot on. The alternative is to set a bias in the course of a few degrees and then run the distance. If at that stage you don't sight the mark the theory is that at least you know which way to turn to find the buoy.

My view is that you are much better off concentrating on getting the course right in the first place than trying to correct the situation later. You can usually steer a more accurate course in a fast boat than you can measure distance covered. Obviously over a short distance, say up to 10 miles, there should be no problem because any errors in the course or distance will still leave you within sighting range of the mark. As the distance between marks increases so can the error — you could be a mile out over a distance of 20 miles. This is about the maximum distance at which you can sight a buoy but it would mean being about 5 degrees off course to get such a large error. The answer is to concentrate on the course steered to keep any errors to a minimum, and have an accurate compass.

When you are making a landfall the situation is different. Here the land will identify itself when you have covered the distance, so you do not need to concern yourself too much with the distance travelled. We have already seen how you can offset the course to one side or the other in order to find a particular spot on a coastline which might appear featureless when you first approach it. This can be a useful technique of second-stage navigation so that you remove the ambiguity from it. The procedure is much the same when you approach a coastline at an oblique angle. Aim to make the landfall at the earliest possible moment and then travel along the coast rather than take the direct route. In this way you will have the reassurance of seeing the land early on and have time to identify features so that, by the time you reach your destination or the next mark, you will be in control of the situation.

Second-stage navigation is really thinking ahead to try to avoid the difficulty

A transit bearing bringing two objects into line can give a useful idea of position at speed, but you still have to judge the distance off. Check these on the chart as part of your preparation.

of not knowing where you are or what to do. It even includes trying to visualise in which direction a mark might be most visible in the particular conditions. Approaching from one direction could make a mark stand out much more clearly than from another under the prevailing conditions, so you might want to bias your course to make sure the mark is on a particular side. An island may not show up against the land, whereas it could be very distinctive against the open sea. So much will depend on the prevailing conditions that it is hard to be specific, but try to consider all the options to arrive at the best solution.

SAFETY MARGINS

When planning your eyeball navigation, always have at the back of your mind the safety margins you are working with. Some of this will come with the second-stage navigation, when you are looking at the chances of finding the mark at the end of a particular leg of a route. But equally you should be looking at the margins in relation to the navigation dangers you are passing. For instance, you should consider whether the one mile distance off the sandbank you will pass is adequate bearing in mind the distance that will be covered before you get to the area. If it is 20 miles away then a one mile margin might not be enough because you cannot guarantee that the course will be that

The basic ingredients for eyeball navigation: a chart, compass, log and echo sounder. Here you have everything at your fingertips and can operate efficiently.

accurate or that there is a buoy marking the sandbank to give you early warning. Over a shorter distance you can reduce the margins because you know that you will only be a limited distance off course.

You may be able to improve on the accuracy because there is land behind the sandbank which will have identifiable features. These can be used to give you a clearer picture of the course you are following as you approach the sandbank. Will there be some of the other features we have already discussed, such as surf breaking on the sandbank, to give early warning of your approach to the danger?

With eyeball navigation there are rarely any hard and fast rules except those of setting the initial course and distance and carrying out a form of mental dead reckoning.

With the speeds which are now being achieved in offshore racing of over 100 mph you have to be confident of high speed navigation because there may be only 20 or 30 seconds from the time you see a mark before you round it. The margins are small but they are acceptable because you are racing. In high speed cruising you want greater margins of safety and, of course, time is on your side because generally you will be travelling much slower.

Despite the slower speed, your safety margins in navigation are largely those found by careful preparation and in weighing up the best course to follow in the circumstances. This will take into account all the varying and sometimes conflicting factors which you have to face to arrive at the best solution. Always bear in mind that almost nothing in eyeball navigation is absolute, so try to allow for margins of safety when things don't work out as expected.

The compass and speed information are the best you have, so try to understand what their accuracy and limitations are. Then you can supplement them with the variety of information from other sources. Eyeball navigation is almost like a return to the basic navigation of hundreds of years ago, only now it is being employed at much higher speeds. Now you need to add the essential ingredient of concentration to make it work – and it cannot be emphasised how important that ingredient is to make it a success.

4 Electronic navigation

You will have appreciated from the last chapter that eyeball navigation has its limitations. In fine conditions with slight seas you can cope, but with the added dimensions of poor visibility, night time or rougher seas then your navigation skills can become stretched. You may be able to cope with the difficulties but at high speeds there can be a considerable element of doubt about the navigation. This is where modern electronic systems can take over to provide answers with a consistency and at a level of convenience which simply cannot be matched by eyeball navigation.

Marine electronics for navigation have grown up with a bad reputation. There is a myth that they are unreliable, that the information cannot be trusted and that if you use electronic equipment you must use all the traditional methods of navigation as well. All of this reflects an attitude which has persisted from the early days when much of it was true, even though the electronics have since changed dramatically.

Much of the unreliability of electronic equipment is due to this very attitude. If you feel that the information being given out is not to be entirely trusted then you will probably adopt a rather casual attitude towards the equipment. If you do not fully understand the systems and how they work, or appreciate the levels of accuracy and the areas and situations where unreliability can occur, or, perhaps most importantly, do not install the equipment to the highest standards, sooner or later it will probably let you down, thus perpetuating the myth.

We will look at installation and other factors later in the book but it is important to appreciate that modern electronics can be extremely reliable, even under the arduous conditions of fast boating. Buy good equipment and install it properly and you open the door to a new world of navigation information which is sheer luxury compared with what was available in the past. With the speed of fast boats rising, this high quality information available from electronics more than compensates for the higher speeds achieved. Just when eyeball navigation was starting to run out of steam, making it difficult to cope with the speed potential of many modern fast boats, electronics have come along to provide the solution. The fast boat navigator should embrace electronics like a friend, get to know and understand them and welcome a new world of high speed accurate navigation.

Electronic navigation has gone through and is still going through a period of change. In the early days there were very basic systems such as radio direction-finding and Consol. These have almost disappeared in favour of the ground based systems, Loran and Decca Navigator. The early versions of these systems have given way to more sophisticated and accurate versions, but these systems still only give local coverage, if a range of 1,000 miles can be considered local. Two world-wide systems were also introduced, Omega and Transit satellite navigation, which were of limited use for fast boats. Omega was an ocean navigation system with poor accuracy for coastal work, whilst Transit, with updates only once an hour or so, was virtually useless for fast craft.

Today Loran C and Decca Navigator have been the primary systems for high speed navigation in the areas where coverage is available. Now a new satellite navigation system, Navstar GPS, is taking over and is destined to become the primary navigation system for fast boats. World-wide in coverage, operational continuously 24 hours a day and with high levels of accuracy, GPS (Global Positioning System) is the answer to the navigator's prayers and will create a revolution in navigation. For the fast boat navigator GPS will open up a new world of navigation where electronics should be able to play a full role without reservations about reliability and accuracy.

LORAN C AND DECCA NAVIGATOR

There are many similarities between Loran C and Decca Navigator. They are both hyperbolic systems using transmissions from shore-based transmitters which are received on board, processed and used to determine the position. There are two major differences between the two, however. Loran C uses time differences between transmitted signals to establish the position, whilst Decca uses phase difference measurements. The other major difference is that Loran C operates over longer ranges than Decca, up to 1,000 miles or more from the master transmitter, whilst the Decca range is less than half that figure.

This is not intended to be a comparison between the two. In general the coverage doesn't overlap, so you will have no choice about which of these systems to use. From an operational point of view, there is little difference between the two and the potential errors and weaknesses are generally common to both. It is essential that you understand these weaknesses so that you can use the systems intelligently and only place reliance on the given positions when this is justified.

Loran C and Decca both operate from signals sent out from transmitters which are organised in chains. A chain will comprise a master and two or more

Route planning with a Decca Navigator receiver. Here the latitude and longitude of the waypoints are entered into the receiver in harbour for use at sea. (Photo: Racal Marine.)

slaves. With Loran C the master transmitter triggers a pulse which is followed by pulses sent out from the slaves. The on-board receiver picks up the pulses from the different transmitters and measures the time difference between receiving the different pulses. With Decca the signal is transmitted on a continuous basis with careful phase alignment between the different trans-missions. The receiver measures the phase difference and this difference – or the time difference in the case of Loran C – means that the receiver must be on a particular position line. The difference measured between the master and another slave will give a second position line, and where the two position lines cross is the position of the vessel. Decca and Loran are hyperbolic navigation systems, the term deriving from the shape of the position lines when plotted on the chart.

So far, so good, and in a perfect world that would be the end of the story, but unfortunately the transmitted signals are affected by outside influences which distort the position lines and reduce the accuracy unless corrections are applied. These come in two forms, fixed and variable errors. The former, as their name implies, don't change and, once determined, can be applied as a matter of course. Many modern receivers have these fixed errors applied automatically and this is a point to check. The fixed errors are mainly caused by the transmitted signal passing over land which affects the propagation of the transmitted signal.

Much more of a problem are the variable errors. These generally change with the time of day and also with location. The low frequency radio transmissions are affected by the height of the ionosphere which varies between night and day. In general the errors are less in the daytime than at night, but the transition between day and night can also cause variations in the errors outside the more regular pattern. Both fixed and variable errors can be found from tables issued by relevant authorities. In the case of Decca this is Racal Marine Ltd, and for Loran C it is the US Coast Guard. The equipment manufacturers should also be able to help.

USING DECCA AND LORAN

The traditional way of using Decca and Loran was to take the readings of phase or time difference and plot them on specially prepared charts which had the position line pattern superimposed on them. The advanced processing power of the modern computer-based receivers allowed these time and phase differences to be changed into latitude and longitude read-outs so that the special charts were no longer required for plotting. With latitude and longitude available it was then possible to use the receivers for waypoint navigation, with presentations of course and distance to go to the next waypoint and the cross track error.

This type of receiver gives the fast boat navigator virtually all the information he needs – but what about these errors? They don't disappear just because you have converted them into latitude and longitude. However, it becomes harder to apply them because they tend to be tabled in the form of corrections to the time or phase difference readings.

The fixed errors may be applied automatically, but check this with the handbook or with the manufacturers. If not, the corrections can be found in information issued by the system operators, the US Coast Guard for Loran, and Racal Marine Ltd for Decca. Most receivers have a facility to apply the basic corrections to the time or phase difference readings, but if they don't then you will have problems because in general you can't apply them to latitude and longitude. Because you can't apply the corrections this means you must allow for greater position inaccuracies when using these systems.

A Loran C receiver which needs to be linked to a plotter for best results. The latitude and longitude on their own are meaningless unless plotted on a chart, which is difficult to do in a fast boat. (Photo: Navstar.)

Variable errors have to be applied manually if possible. An indication of the expected variable errors can be found from the same sources as the fixed errors. They have been worked out from experience, but because they are variable they will be less accurate than the fixed errors and it is these variable errors which mainly account for the level of accuracy that is available. The accuracy will also vary with distance from the transmitters: the closer you are the better the accuracy because the position lines are closer together. Move away and the wider spacing of the position lines means that the same error in time or phase difference will cover a greater distance, increasing the error effect.

This means that you really need to understand the geometry of the chain in order to appreciate the effect of errors, but there are other good reasons to have a map of the transmitter layout. If you study such a map you will see that generally in the areas covered by the master and slave transmitters the hyperbolic position lines are reasonably close together, meaning that a large change in the Decca or Loran readings will have a comparatively small effect on the position. You will also notice that the various position lines cross reasonably close to a right angle, the prerequisite for a good fix. Look further away from the transmitters and not only do the lines fan out but the angle of crossing between the position lines gets smaller. Both of these features will exaggerate any errors so that the accuracy will be reduced.

Now look at what happens in what is called the base line extension area. This is where a line joining the master and a slave passes outside the area encompassed by the transmitters. It is a pretty dead area as far as getting any worthwhile position is concerned. There is very little change in the values over large distances so accuracy here can be very poor. You can find another dead area when you are very close to a transmitter, and as these are often located on the coast to reduce the land effect errors, you have to watch out for this. The dead area could extend up to 10 miles from the transmitter.

You can see from this why it is important to have a map with you showing the layout of the chain. With Loran, the transmitters are generally very widely spaced, 500 miles or more apart, so you are unlikely to see any dramatic changes even when you are covering considerable distances in a fast boat. With Decca Navigator you could easily cover a major part of a chain in a day's run in a fast boat, so you could expect different accuracies and errors to occur in the short term.

Because of the latitude and longitude read-out you will get little indication of the varying errors from the receiver itself, although some receivers do give an idea of the accuracy which might be obtained based on the geographical position of the receiver. Most receivers can let you know what the signal-to-noise ratio is, which is a guide to the strength of the incoming signals and gives a clue to their reliability. If you operate your boat in a fairly compact area, then you will quickly become accustomed to the changes in signal and accuracy that you can expect, but on a long passage you should watch the situation carefully and perhaps add the study of the chain pattern to your list of preparatory work.

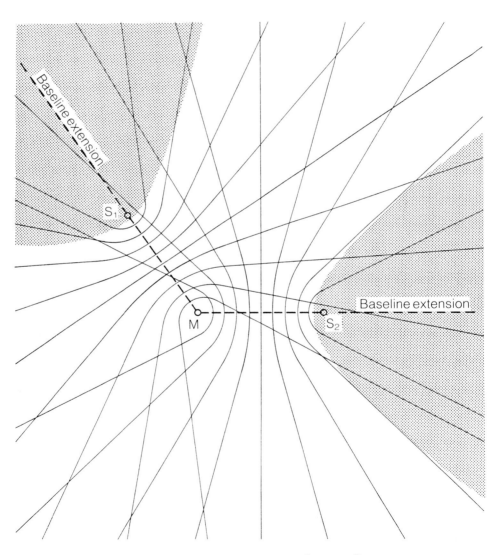

The master and secondary transmitters and the pattern of position lines they generate. The areas where the position lines cross at small angles will not give accurate positions. This is worst at the extensions of the base lines joining the transmitters (shown shaded).

Unfortunately the story doesn't end there – there are still more problems that you have to watch out for. The effect of land on the transmitted signals has already been mentioned so it shouldn't come as a surprise to find that there can be problems using these systems in narrow channels or areas surrounded by land. This is a greater problem with Decca than with Loran, and in severe cases where the water is bounded by high land you can lose the signal to the point where the receiver readings can be valueless. It is usually a temporary problem, and full service is resumed when you get out into open water. The fact that you are close to land allows eyeball navigation to take over, but in fog you could find yourself without the electronic help you were banking on.

Electrical storms are another factor which can put your Loran or Decca receiver off course. In my experience, it is Loran receivers which are more susceptible to this interference, and a severe electrical storm can leave you without position information. This problem becomes more severe if you are some way from the transmitters and the signal is weak. It can be disconcerting to find that you have no position information with all that thunder and lightning about and you suspect that the receiver may have been permanently damaged. My experience of many such storms is that the receiver has always come back on line, so this can be considered a temporary interruption to the service.

From all this you may wonder if a Decca or Loran receiver is worthwhile, but I have no hesitation in recommending them to fast boat navigators. They give so much useful information – which may not be available from any other source – that they are easy to justify. Knowing the course and distance to the next waypoint and the cross track error enables you to navigate at high speed with a degree of confidence which you will rarely have with eyeball navigation. The important thing to remember is that there can be errors in the system which can reduce its accuracy so don't navigate to too fine a margin. Always keep something in hand in case the errors are larger than you think and in this way you will build up a comfortable relationship with the electronic receiver.

SELECTING A RECEIVER

The range of receivers on the market for both Loran and Decca varies enormously both in quality and price. It is often difficult to see what you get by paying extra money, but the difference is generally in the improved software of the computer and in the better quality of the hardware which will probably give it a better chance of survival in the harsh fast boat environment. Don't be bemused by the many fancy features which are often the only outward sign of the higher cost. It is quite easy for a manufacturer to build in all sorts of extras into the software, processing the raw information to produce extra information which you will probably never use. Much more important to you is a large clear display which will be easy to read when the boat is bouncing about, good night-time lighting which will enable you to read the display clearly at night but which also has a dimming facility, and single button selection of different information pages.

The main information you will be interested in will be the course and distance to the next waypoint and the cross track error. Ideally these should all come up on the one display so that you don't have to continually switch from one to the other. Another page should show the latitude and longitude (although you won't be able to do much with it at speed) and a third should indicate the waypoint you are heading for. Perhaps more important than these last two pages are ones showing the signal-to-noise ratio and any page which gives some idea of accuracy. Some receivers give an indication of the reliability which can be placed on the information being presented, maybe a display indicator or a light system. This is a useful check, but understand how it works and on what it bases its information before you rely on it.

The other point to watch for when choosing a receiver is whether it will cope with the speed at which the boat is likely to travel. Some receivers run out of steam at speeds over 20 knots and do not update quickly enough to cope with higher speeds. This means that the receiver becomes confused and sends out alarm signals. Modern receivers tend to be better in this respect and can cope with higher speeds, but once you start travelling at over 40 knots you may have to resort to those receivers designed for aircraft use. There are a growing number of these appearing on the marine market, suitably packaged for the different environment, and they are good for high speed work provided they meet the other requirements of ease of use, examined above.

SATELLITE NAVIGATION

The Transit satellite system only updates every hour or so – maybe at even longer intervals. On top of this it needs a compass and log input to achieve reasonable accuracy, and a good log input is not always available on a fast boat. This means that Transit has virtually no application on fast boats, although I have used it on Atlantic crossings as a back up system. It is the new satellite system, Navstar GPS, which holds out much more promise as a high speed navigation system. In years to come it will probably take over from Decca and Loran for fast boat navigation, mainly because it is much less prone to errors and because it will give consistently high accuracy.

GPS is scheduled to become fully operational by 1992. By that time the eighteen Block II satellites will all be orbiting the earth at a height of 22,000 miles, going around the earth approximately twice a day on elliptical orbits. Before that date there will probably be full coverage for the marine user because there are a number of experimental Block I satellites in orbit and these will combine with the new satellites being launched to give useful coverage.

The GPS system demonstrates the capabilities of modern technology to the full. Even though the satellites are a long way from earth, their orbits are plotted very accurately and the position of a receiver is found by measuring the range from the satellites which are in 'view'. The range is measured with extreme accuracy so that position can be determined to an accuracy of about 10 yards. That may sound amazing and GPS is a system with tremendous capabilities, but now let's talk about the drawbacks.

Like most of the electronic navigation systems GPS is starting off life as a military system. No other organisation could afford the huge costs involved in getting the system operational, but for the first time commercial requirements are being considered from the outset and the system, or at least some of it, will be available to commercial users from the word go. This is where the main

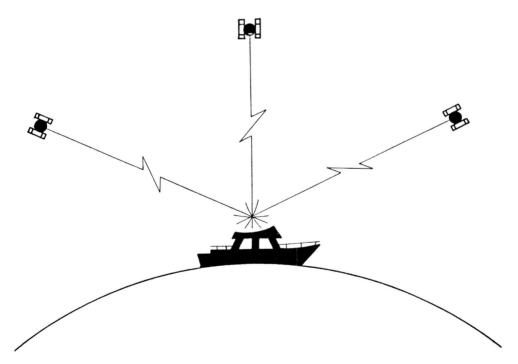

GPS picks up signals from three or more satellites, measures the ranges and translates them into a position. Because at least three satellites are always 'in view' position fixing is continuous.

drawback lies because the US military, who are paying for the system, are reluctant to make this high accuracy available to all users so it will be reserved mainly for the military.

Commercial users will have to make do with a considerably reduced

A compact GPS receiver into which you can enter the names of waypoints to reduce the likelihood of mistakes. This unit is portable with its own batteries which reduce the possibility of failing, but for use in a fast boat it will need fixing down. (Photo: Magellan.)

accuracy; currently the figure being offered is around 100 yards. This compares favourably with the general accuracy available from Loran or Decca in good areas, so the navigator will not be any worse off. Indeed he will gain considerably from the consistent performance of GPS, which means that there are no fixed or variable errors of any significance and the system is virtually unaffected by weather conditions. There is also the benefit that the system is available world-wide, although this will benefit very few navigators except for the fact that it will bring electronic navigation to many areas not previously covered as far as fast boat navigation is concerned.

The system is still being developed, particularly with regard to commercial usage, and one possibility is that the system could eventually be integrated with a similar Russian system, Glonass, also under development. It is doubtful whether full integration will take place because of incompatibility, but one benefit of the collaboration could be a dramatic shortening of the warning time if a satellite goes down. Such a failure could seriously affect the integrity of the position received or mean that you get no position at all. Current plans only call for a leisurely warning an hour or more after the event. Collaboration with the Russians could bring the warning time down to a matter of seconds, an improvement of great benefit to commercial aircraft and to fast boats. If you are going to place heavy reliance on a navigation system, then you do need early warning of any system failure.

Because of the military implications associated with GPS plans have been developed for commercial systems using satellites, but the future of these seems to be uncertain, at least until GPS is up and running. However things develop, it seems certain that the future of high speed navigation lies with satellites. The cost of receivers will come down to a figure comparable with current Decca or Loran receivers which will open up the way to widespread use. Loran will continue as a back-up system at least until the turn of the century, but the future of Decca Navigator is less certain and it faces the possibility of being replaced by Loran in Northern Europe.

NAVIGATING WITH GPS

Current GPS receivers resemble Loran and Decca receivers very closely in most respects, one notable difference being price, although this is coming down all the time. There is a numeric keyboard for entering data and dedicated push buttons for selecting what is displayed. At the time of writing the system was not fully operational, but one major difference is that you have one information page which can be called up to show when the next position fixes will be available. Routes and waypoints can be fed in and another of the main differences is that there is no need to have a forecast of the accuracy of the receiver because the information is good and reliable.

When it comes to using a GPS receiver on a fast boat life will be a lot easier once the full satellite coverage is available. You will not have to worry about the accuracy levels so you will be able to plan your electronic navigation much more precisely. The quoted accuracy level of 100 yards is likely to be the worst that you will find, so you will not have to allow the same margins as you would with Loran or Decca where there are variable errors. As you become familiar with GPS the main problem you are likely to have to face is complacency. The consistent performance could lead you into the trap of believing that the GPS receiver is infallible. Believe that and sooner or later you will be heading for trouble; you must never neglect the basic rule of navigation – caution – that allows for things going wrong.

GPS is set to revolutionise powerboat navigation, not so much because of changes in the basic techniques of navigation, but because of a growing reliance on electronics. The intrinsic possibility of errors in Loran C and Decca Navigator do not encourage full reliance on the systems, but GPS could change all that. A growing dependence on electronic position fixing information of high quality will form the basis of integrated navigation systems which will allow confident navigation at high speed and in difficult conditions. An essential part of this integration will be electronic charts and plotters.

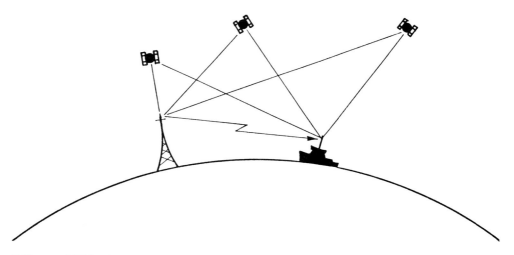

Differential GPS, where signals are received on board and on shore. The position of the receiver on shore is accurately known, so corrections can be sent from here to the on-board receiver to upgrade the quality of the position.

ELECTRONIC CHARTS AND PLOTTERS

In high speed navigation we have already come across the fact that latitude and longitude positions on their own are not much use. They have to be transferred to the chart to give useful information, but chartwork is difficult to carry out in the high speed environment. This is where electronic charts and plotters come in; they are the logical extension of electronic navigation at high speed.

The main advantage is in the way in which the information is presented. Digital information can be hard to assess at high speed even when it is in the form of course and distance to the next waypoint and cross track error. You still have to visualise these figures in relation to the chart and there is the possibility of making mistakes. The electronic chart or plotter presents a graphic picture of the navigation which is easy to interpret – and this is a real-time picture, continuously updated to show what is happening.

The difference between plotters and charts is that the plotter has only course and track information on it whilst the electronic chart combines this with chart information to give a more complete picture.

Plotters

Let us first of all look at plotters which are the simplest form of display. There are a wide variety of plotters on the market and the distinction between plotters and electronic charts is often blurred. The plotter screen generally has a basic latitude and longitude grid superimposed and this is invariably on the Mercator projection so that you have the same distortion as is found on the paper chart, the scale varying with latitude. Plotters vary in their capability, but those operating in conjunction with a position-fixing receiver of the same manufacture invariably allow a two-way exchange of information. Waypoints pinpointed on the plotter can be put into the memory of the position-fixing receiver and vice versa. Having selected a waypoint or route you want to follow, you can display it on the plotter screen as a line showing the desired track.

Now with the receiver supplying position information, the position of the vessel is shown on the plotter screen. Immediately you have a picture of where you are in relation to where you want to be. In particular you can see whether you are one side or the other of the selected track, so it is easy to take corrective action. Limited chart information can usually be added to the plotter screen in the form of marks which can represent buoys or headlands, so you can have a more complete picture of the situation. In many cases it is possible to introduce a stylised coastline representation, but this can mean quite a bit of plotting work.

Apart from showing the required and actual courses, one of the main benefits of the plotter display is its ability to show up immediately any problems with the navigation receiver. If you are steering a straight course and the plotter shows a dip in the course, then you will immediately suspect the information from the receiver. Variations in the track shown in this way can be particularly useful when you are using Loran or Decca, giving a guide to the quality of the information being received. Small variations will indicate the level of accuracy that can be anticipated, whilst any major variation could indicate a problem with the receiver or with the transmitting system. On the plotter these variations would show up immediately in a way which might not be apparent if you were looking at a digital display only.

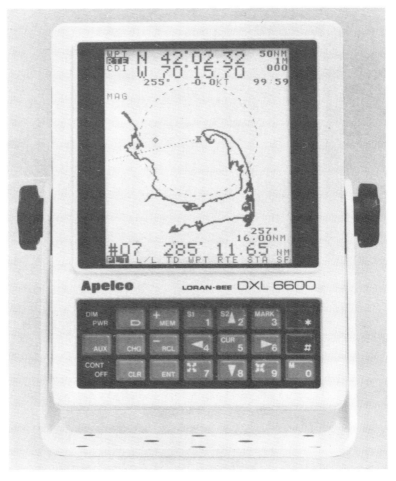

A combined Loran C receiver and mini plotter suitable for small powerboats. This unit uses an LCD display which is generally reliable at sea. (Photo: Apelco.)

The display on the plotter screen is always history, showing where you have been rather than where you are going. To a navigator this reveals one of the weaknesses of the plotter because you are much more interested in where you are going. Indeed the historical track has very little relevance, except that it does enable you to project ahead mentally to show where your track will take you. This in turn can only be related to the next waypoint and you then have to refer to the paper chart to see where that waypoint might be in relation to navigation dangers.

You can use the track on the plotter to make course variations in order to keep the track you are making good in line with the route you want to follow. This can be done manually by making course alterations when you see the track and the route diverging. With some systems it is possible to do this automatically, linking the navigation receiver and the plotter to an autopilot. The autopilot is instructed to maintain a steady course in the normal way, but it can also be instructed to make alterations based on variations in the cross track error. With this ability to sense and correct cross track errors of very small magnitude, the vessel can be kept close to the desired track in a way which would be difficult with manual control. Because you have already compared the track on the plotter with the same track on the paper chart you can navigate with confidence, knowing that you are not deviating from the chosen path.

The plotter obviously has its limitations even though some of the units on the market are quite sophisticated. It is generally the lack of navigation information on the display which creates these limitations, so the plotter is really an intermediate stage in the development of the display of navigation information. The electronic chart is the next step forward.

Electronic charts
The electronic chart is a plotter display combined with a display of chart information. One look at a paper chart shows that a wealth of information is contained on one sheet of paper, and the main problem facing the electronic chart manufacturers is how much of that information can be transferred to the electronic screen, and in what form. There is a wide variety of electronic chart systems on the market ranging from those with a simple representation of the coastline to those which display an authentic representation of the paper chart, and of course many degrees of sophistication in between. The choice is wide and we will look at this in more detail in a later chapter, but a basic understanding of the differences will help to put electronic navigation into perspective.

The simple type of electronic chart display where just the coastline and major navigation marks are shown is a much more comforting picture for the navigator than the basic plotter display. It shows the route in relation to the coast and gives the navigator a means of checking that the waypoints have been plotted correctly. By seeing the track moving across the screen in relation to the coastline, this type of chart carries out automatically the type of plotting the navigator would do on a paper chart if the conditions allowed. This is reassuring, but it doesn't tell the whole story because the display may not show navigation dangers under or on the water, which can be the more important ones.

The basic coastline display is aimed at simplicity. Some manufacturers of electronic charts do, however, allow the user to add a variety of other information to the display so that they can, to a certain extent, tailor the display to suit their particular navigation requirements. This extra information is available in the form of electronic 'pages', and calling up a particular display is rather like putting a transparent overlay on the paper chart. One 'page' for instance might show the buoyage for the area, and another could show depth contours. Around six pages of additional information are normally available on this type of electronic chart, though if you use them all, the screen can become almost saturated with information and very difficult to understand.

This type of electronic chart system is popular because it can be used with comparatively low cost equipment, particularly in terms of information storage. The cost can also be kept low by using monochrome displays, but there are limits to what can be shown and there is always the risk that you will take the display at face value, assuming that there is nothing else of consequence to worry about and forgetting that there are other pages of information stored away which will tell the full story. This could be a particular problem when you are navigating under the stress of very high speed or in rough seas.

The more sophisticated electronic displays use colour which allows more information to be displayed within a given space on the screen. One information storage system uses laser discs and the storage capacity here is such that actual photographs of the paper chart can be stored and called up as required. This is a major step forward, but for high speed navigation it is still not the complete answer. We have seen in an earlier chapter how the paper chart needs to be enhanced with pencil marks to make it suitable for high speed work. You really need the same facility with these electronic displays of the chart if you are to be able to concentrate on the important features and not have a screen in front of you which can become a meaningless blur at high speed.

The current technology of electronic chart systems still leaves much to be desired as far as high speed navigation is concerned, but this should not put you off. Even with their limitations, electronic charts present information to you at high speed in a way which is not possible by manual means and this represents a great step forward, giving you real-time information of great value. The important thing is to be aware of the limitations of the system so that you don't get caught out by assuming too much from the information presented.

LIMITATIONS OF ELECTRONIC NAVIGATION

Electronic navigation is a major step forward because it tells you with a considerable degree of certainty where you are. The navigators of old would think that was the end of the story, because once you know where you are, you can work out everything else. This assumes the luxury of time, the one thing you don't have on a fast boat. However, it is possible to compensate for that to a certain extent by preparation, and electronic systems will, in the future, allow us to have a much better control over the navigation situation in real time,

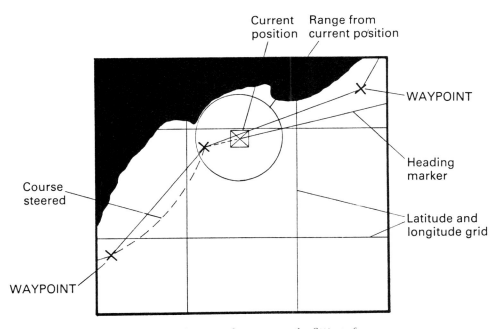

An ideal electronic chart display. The main features are the fitting of a range marker and heading marker, the latter showing where you are going, which is of much more interest to the navigator.

because accurate positions will be available and displays will show the navigation situation in a way which will be easy to assess.

There are two main limitations to electronic navigation. One is that you want to know the accuracy of the information which is being presented to you so that you can make considered judgements about how you will use it. The other, which is related, is that you are much more interested in where you are going than in where you have come from, and electronic navigation is only now starting to present information in a way which is more usable to the high speed navigator.

On the first of these points, the temptation is to take the information presented by the electronic systems for granted. When a display shows latitude and longitude to two decimal places of minutes, it is quite hard to come up with a rational thought which disputes the position. It is presented in such a positive way that it allows little room for argument and yet, as we have seen in the sections on Loran and Decca, there can be considerable errors in the position given under some circumstances. Your visual assessment of the position using eyeball navigation is unlikely to be any more accurate and so you are left with the dilemma of knowing that there could be inaccuracies but not knowing whether they do exist or what they might be.

The answer to the dilemma is caution and constant checking. The accuracy of the Loran and Decca positions can be checked each time you pass a buoy or a fixed navigation mark. The plotter or electronic chart is the ideal way to make the check because you can immediately see the position where you would be against the position shown, provided the mark has been plotted. You can do the same by comparing the latitude and longitude positions, but it is not so easy to imagine the bearing and distance of the error. Evaluating the error in this way gives you a correction which should be valid for 30 miles or more from that position, but it may not remain valid if you are close to land, particularly under high cliffs or hills.

Some electronic chart systems allow errors determined in this way to be applied automatically as corrections to the position, so that the actual position plotted on the screen has better accuracy. It seems a logical step to take, but take care for two reasons. First, there is a temptation to make the initial correction when you are in harbour, where the incoming signal could be affected by dockside installations, thus giving you a false correction for open waters. Secondly, you could go on for mile after mile using the same correction, so it is important to take every opportunity to update the correction as you pass buoys or other marks.

Now let us turn to where you are going. What you want to know is how your present course shapes up to the land and other navigation marks around you.

Electronic position-fixing systems do this to some extent by giving you the course and distance to the next waypoint and the cross track error. This helps you to build up a mental picture of the situation, but it only relates this to the waypoint and not to the land and sea around you. The electronic chart can be a help in this respect because it shows your track, but it doesn't give a complete picture because there is no heading marker to show where you are going. You can mentally extend the track, but electronic chart systems linked to a compass to show the heading are the next step in development. Another possibility is for the heading marker to correspond to the course made good obtained from the electronic position-fixing receiver. Either of these systems would help to resolve this situation and they will be on the market soon.

Radar can provide many of these answers already and we will look at this in the next chapter, but it should be obvious that no one piece of electronics can give the high speed navigator all he wants. The way ahead lies in the integration of various systems to provide the navigator with the full electronic picture of his surroundings.

DIFFERENTIAL NAVIGATION

In the last section we looked at techniques of ascertaining precisely where the boat is, finding out the errors of the electronic systems and applying them to upgrade the accuracy of the positions in the future. This is a type of differential navigation applied on a very local basis, but in the future differential systems could have a wider impact on navigation, particularly when GPS comes into full operation.

The accuracy of GPS is being deliberately downgraded to protect the military applications of the system, but existing differential systems working with GPS have shown how the accuracy can be restored almost to the level prevailing before downgrading. It may seem a nonsensical approach to navigation to introduce errors deliberately and then develop a system to correct them, but until the military change their minds we have to live with this, and differential systems could give you GPS results with an accuracy of 5–10 yards which no fast boat navigator is going to argue about.

The system works by having a GPS receiver placed in a location which has been determined to a high level of accuracy. When the readings of the receiver are compared with the known position, the errors can be determined. Now these errors have to be relayed to vessels at sea and this is done by using radio transmissions, often using blank sections of transmissions already in existence such as radio beacons. The corrections are received on board and are applied automatically to the GPS receiver to give much higher accuracy.

GPS differential systems are already in existence and the technology is well proven. Tests have shown that the corrections determined at one location can be valid up to 1,000 miles or more from that position, so one system could cover a wide area. Similar systems have been tried with Loran, but here the corrections are much more local, so that a Loran differential system would only be valid for perhaps 50 miles from the base station depending on the local topography.

In the interim stage before GPS is fully available there is an alternative form of differential navigation receiver available. This is a combination Loran/GPS or Decca GPS receiver which works on GPS when it is available and then automatically switches to Loran or Decca at other times. When the GPS signals are available, the Loran/Decca and GPS positions are compared and, assuming that GPS is accurate, the corrections to upgrade the Loran/Decca positions are computed and automatically applied. This gives better accuracy all round, but in using such a receiver you must be aware that corrections are applied automatically so do not apply them manually as well.

Differential systems introduced for GPS are probably only a temporary requirement. When the military appreciate that the downgrading can be overridden in this way on a regular basis they may well abandon or at least reduce the downgrading of the accuracy. Then with high accuracy available to all we will truly be on the brink of a navigation revolution which will take a great deal of the guesswork and worry out of high speed navigation.

REDUNDANCY

If you are going to rely heavily on electronics for fast boat navigation, then you must have reliability. Much can be done to achieve this by careful installation and by the design of the receiver itself but a failure could leave you in difficulties. The logical next step is to have two receivers in case one fails. This also allows you to check the readings of one against the other but if they show different readings which one do you believe? If you take this argument to its logical conclusion you need three receivers. This will allow a 'voting' system to operate with the two receivers showing the same reading being the ones to rely on.

This is the way aircraft approach the use of electronics for navigation and in fast boats you need to adopt the same technique if you want to place full reliance on electronics. I have no doubt that at some time in the future it will be common to have two or more receivers on board to allow for failures, and this built-in redundancy will open up the way to a new era of electronic navigation. Fast boats will probably be the first to use multiple receivers because they will become the first to place full dependence on electronics for navigation. Once GPS is fully established the door will be open for this approach, but it will be necessary to build a small printer into the system in order to have a position print-out at regular intervals. From this print-out it would be possible to resort to basic slow speed navigation techniques if there was a total electronic failure.

5 Radar

Of all the pieces of electronic equipment which it is possible to carry on board a fast boat there is no doubt that if you had to reduce it to one then radar would be the first choice. Amongst electronics for fast boats radar is unique because it not only shows you where you are in relation to your surroudings, but perhaps much more importantly it shows you where you are going. On a fast boat your present position is very quickly history and, as navigator, where you are going is much more important than where you are at any particular time. Radar gives you this information via the heading marker on the screen, information which is valuable both in fine weather and in poor visibility. Of course the other aspect of radar that can be vitally important in poor visibility is its capability of showing the locations of other vessels around you so that you can carry out collision avoidance. Once again radar is unique in this respect and so a radar set on a fast boat certainly earns its keep.

With all this potential radar promises a great deal to the navigator, but unfortunately it never quite lives up to its promise. The information shown on the radar display must be treated with a degree of caution. It rarely gives you the apparently precise information available from other electronic navigation instruments. With radar there are times when you have to coax information out of the set, and indeed an important factor in the operation of any radar set is the interaction which is necessary between the operator and the display. Only in this way can you be aware of the inadequacies of or omissions from the display, whilst at the same time know which information can be relied on and which you have to treat with an element of caution. With radar you have to worry not so much about the information which you can see on the screen but about that which could be missing, such as small boats or areas of land hidden from view. If you are going to cope with these omissions you have to understand just how the radar works and how it can be used to get the best possible quality of information. This relationship or interaction between the user and the display is particularly important on fast boats where the apparent movement on the radar display is rapid and changes can occur very quickly. You therefore have to remain on top of the situation the whole time.

With the map-like display of radar it is very easy to take what you see at face value. Because the display is shown in plan view it is very easy to imagine that what you have displayed is a bird's eye of the whole navigation environment around you. Of course this is not the case because the radar scanner which is picking up the information is located not very far above your head. To get a true idea of how the radar picture is developed you have to imagine yourself in the position of the radar scanner turning round and viewing the horizon through 360 degrees; what you see is what is shown on the radar display. However, this is only part of the story because the radar has one feature which is not available to the human eye and that is the ability to measure distances accurately. This enables the radar to differentiate between targets which appear to merge when viewed by the human eye, but which on the radar display could well be separated by some distance. This is a very valuable feature which can enable harbour entrances to show up on radar when they are virtually invisible to the human eye, and it can give a much better picture of the layout of the land features. Again, because of the plan display of the radar there is a strong temptation to compare it with the features seen on the chart, but of course these two may not provide the same picture because some features of the land may well be hidden from the scanner's view by other land features in front of them.

The low viewpoint of the radar scanner compared with the bird's eye presentation of the chart means that the land features on the radar will tend to unfold as you progress along the coast rather than be fully visible at one time. This will be particularly evident as you pass a headland, when the features on the far side may be invisible until you round the headland. It is therefore very important to understand the concept of just how the radar views the targets around it so that you can appreciate what might or might not show up.

Another aspect of radar that has to be considered is that of the relative motion of the radar display. Many users find it hard to grasp this aspect of radar whereby 'own ship' stays in the centre of the screen so that the land moves past you rather than you moving past the land. The relationship of 'own ship' and the land is not so difficult to understand, but problems can occur when trying to relate relative motion to vessel targets. These targets appear to move on the screen with a combination of the speed and course of your own vessel as well as their own, and this makes it quite hard to appreciate just how they are moving when you are trying to decide collision avoidance tactics.

True motion radars are available but these tend to be for larger craft. These have your own vessel's speed and course fed into the radar's computer so that you can see your vessel moving across the screen. The land stays still and other vessels move according to their true course and speed. Such a radar display is much easier to understand and it makes collision avoidance easier, but the sets tend to be large and complex and are rarely fitted to small, fast craft. This means that the fast boat navigator is restricted to a relative motion radar in most cases; certainly in this chapter these are the radars we will consider primarily.

The problems of using such a radar can appear quite daunting at first. However, once you grasp the way it operates and gain experience in its use, then the radar can present the navigator with a whole host of extremely valuable information. This can enable him to keep on top of the navigation situation at times when he may find himself very short of alternative information, particularly in poor visibility.

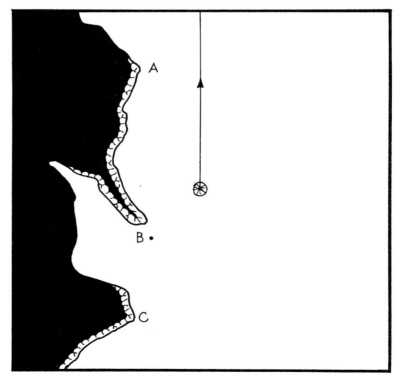

The land beyond the headlands A and C will be hidden from view on the radar, as will the land inside point B.

THE PRINCIPLES OF RADAR

There are four parts to a small boat radar; the transmitter, the scanner, the receiver and the display unit. In most small boat radars these are combined into two units; the transmitter and the scanner, and the display unit and the receiver, an arrangement which makes for simple installation. Combining the scanner and transmitter also ensures that the maximum amount of energy from the transmitter is radiated out through the scanner. The transmitter sends out very short pulses at a very high frequency. The rotating scanner directs these pulses to different points around the horizon and they are reflected back from any solid object which they strike. The reflected signals are collected by the scanner, processed in the receiver and shown on the display as the familiar radar picture.

After sending out the pulse the scanner is then opened for the reception of the returned pulses and such is the speed of the radio waves used for the radar that the pulses go out and back many miles in the very short space of time in which the scanner faces a particular direction.

The length of the transmitted pulse is important because the receiver cannot be opened for reception until the pulse has been transmitted. Here we are only talking about microseconds but you have to remember that the radar pulse travels at the rate of one mile in 6.2 microseconds. The shorter the pulse length, the sooner the receiver is opened for business. Whilst the transmission is going on, nothing can be received and so you have a small dead area around the vessel corresponding to the length of the transmitted pulse.

Typically a pulse length of 0.1 microseconds is used on the shorter radar ranges which is equivalent to about 30 metres. This means that the dead area where no targets will be detected will extend for this distance around the vessel. For longer ranges there is not enough energy in this short pulse and so longer pulse lengths are used, typically having a length of 0.5 microseconds, which will increase the dead area around the vessel to 150 metres. This is not serious when you are using the longer ranges and the switch from one pulse length to another is done automatically as you change the range on the radar control panel.

Another point to consider is the pulse repetition frequency (PRF). There is no point in sending out another pulse from the scanner until the returning pulses from the last transmission have all returned. On short ranges a higher PRF can be tolerated because the pulses do not have very far to travel, and this higher PRF gives a better chance of detecting small targets. On the short ranges PRF is typically around 2,500 pulses per second, whilst on longer ranges this figure is usually halved.

Earlier types of radar use a radial display for the cathode ray (CRT) tube which provides the operator interface. The spokes of this radial display line up with the direction of the scanner which is effectively a time measuring device, so that when the pulse sets out from the scanner, the track of the radial display sets out from the centre travelling at a proportional speed. When a target is intercepted and sends back a return, this is shown on the display as a highlighted area on the radial track out from the centre, equivalent to the distance away from the target.

These radial displays have now been virtually superseded by the raster scan display, and this makes a significant difference to the way the radar operates. Instead of the radar being based on mechanical and electrical/electronic measuring devices, the raster scan radar is almost entirely software based which gives a great deal more scope for the return signal to be processed before being shown on the display screen. The raster scan display, which is in effect a series of horizontal lines rather than the radial lines of the earlier type of display, also allows for digital information as well as track lines and other information to be shown on the screen; indeed the information shown on the screen is only limited by the imagination of the designer.

Small boat radars have gone through a series of developments. Initially they were simply cheap versions of large ship radars from which many of the more sophisticated features had been removed. This didn't make them particularly useful for small boats where these sophisticated features can be quite valuable. Now with the development of the software based raster scan radar, we are seeing a return of many of these features and indeed the small boat radar of today is once more becoming quite sophisticated, which is certainly of tremendous benefit for fast boat operations.

The processing of the raw radar information by the software-based radar receiver can give enormous benefits in terms of the clarity of the display. It means that very weak targets can be enhanced to make them show up more clearly on the screen, but it also allows for random returns, such as might occur from sea clutter, to be decreased in strength so that they don't obliterate other weak targets. Most radar manufacturers have developed their own sophisticated processing methods and it is quite important that you under-stand just what is happening to the raw radar information from the scanner so that you can appreciate just what is being shown on the display. Only in this way will you gain some idea of what targets could be missing from the screen and be in a position to interpret the information in a meaningful way.

Another very valuable feature of the radar scan display is that it is bright enough to be viewed in most daylight conditions. For fast boat users this is extremely useful because it means that you no longer have to peer into a shielding hood to see the screen, and the radar picture can be visible from most parts of the wheelhouse which makes both installation and operation much simpler.

Software-based radars also mean that many of the setting-up procedures are now automatic. The tuning of the receiver to the frequency of the transmitted signal is maintained automatically at the optimum setting on some radars, although manual control is a facility in some cases. The centring of the radar picture with the display is also automatic as is the setting of the heading marker on the zero position. You still have to set the gain and brilliance controls to suit the ambient conditions, but in some cases the sea clutter control is automated, although a manual override is invariably fitted.

RADAR FEATURES

When selecting a radar for use in a fast boat it is quite important to understand just what features you need for this type of use. Modern radars can incorporate a whole host of features which can make them more useful in particular conditions, and with this wide choice an understanding of the beneficial features is necessary. Some of the features allow you to take measurements from the screen whilst others can improve the ability for collision avoidance and assist with navigation.

Measuring range is perhaps one of the most vital features because it is so difficult to do by any other means on board. There are two methods of measuring range by radar. One is with fixed range rings, which on a six mile range could be positioned every mile so that you have a series of concentric rings on the radar display and can interpolate between the rings to get an idea of your distance from any target. Alternatively the variable range marker (VRM) can be controlled by a knob. This ring can be moved inwards or outwards to be settled on a particular target, with the range being read off from a digital display, usually on the screen itself. Some radars have two variable range markers which can be particularly useful during collision avoidance work enabling you to keep track of two different targets at the one time, or to track the movement of a single target. For this type of tracking you invariably use the VRM in conjunction with a variable bearing marker (VBM), this combination enabling you to pinpoint a particular position on the surface of the screen. As with the range markers, often two VBMs are fitted so that you can pinpoint more than one target at a time.

You will notice that any land features close to the heading marker tend to swing backwards and forwards. This is related to the change in heading of the boat itself, to which the radar display is related. If the heading of the boat changes, as it will do continuously during normal steering, then the display will tend to swing backwards and forwards. This means that any readings taken with the variable range marker have to be treated with a degree of caution and you have to try to average out the position of the target you are measuring to get the mean readings.

Any bearings taken with the VBM are relative bearings, in other words they are bearings from the boat's heading. If you want to translate these into a compass bearing, you must apply the boat's head to the relative bearing:

Boat's heading + Bearing taken from VBM = Compass bearing (− 360 degrees if total is over 360)

Because of this complication, bearings taken off the radar screen are rarely used to fix the position on the chart. If you do need to fix a position for any reason then range rings are a much more accurate way of doing so because they are not subject to the variations of the VBM readings.

Some of the more sophisticated radars have a means whereby the datum point for one of the VRM and VBMs can be offcentred. For instance, you could move the centre point from which the range and bearing are measured away from the centre of the display and place it over a target. Then you can measure range and bearing from that target. Alternatively, you could measure the distance of a buoy off a headland so that you can identify the buoy precisely. This is a useful feature but it does tend to add to the complication of the controls, which may not always be a good thing in fast boat operations.

Another way in which the VRM and VBM can be used is to establish guard zones. These are areas which are defined by range and by bearing. If a target enters this guard zone then either a visual or an audio alarm will sound. By being able to set up the guard zone selectively in sectors or by both minimum and maximum range you can reduce the chance of false alarms or intrusions from land targets, and use this feature mainly to alert you to approaching moving targets.

In my experience guard zones are generally very reliable and the tendency is for them to be triggered off by every small target intrusion into the guard zone (even wave returns) so they err on the side of safety. On fast boats targets can approach you at considerable speed, so setting up a guard zone does ensure that you don't miss an approaching target – although one would hope that you are watching the screen sufficiently to see them long before they hit the zone. False alarms on guard zones are reduced by a feature which ensures that a target has to show up on several successive sweeps of the display before it activates the alarm, which reduces the chance of the alarm being set off by wave clutter.

Another useful feature which is often an option is the ability to offset the centre point of the radar. In most circumstances you are not concerned with what is happening astern, so by offsetting the centre you can gain an extended range ahead. This can provide a useful compromise in the display, which is useful for both general navigation as well as collision avoidance.

The radar display is generally circular, but since the screen is usually square or rectangular in shape this leaves the four corners of the display available for showing digital information. An obvious use for these corners is to show range and bearing information, but they also show the scale of the display in use, the distance apart of range rings, and where the radar is linked to position finding information it can also show the actual position and waypoint information. There is a tendency for as much information as possible to be shown on the radar display in an attempt to make this the primary navigation display. However, much of this information repeats what is shown on the position finding equipment anyway; moreover the information is very small in size and thus is not always easy to read in a bouncing fast boat.

A feature of some small radars these days is the ability to stabilise the radar display north up. Interfacing the radar with a compass is useful if you want stability in the VRM but perhaps the greatest advantage of this type of display is that it becomes comparable with that of the electronic chart; with both these showing north up it is possible to make direct comparisons between the two and identify navigation features rapidly. Perhaps the disadvantage of the north-up display is that the heading marker may be in any position on the screen, making it harder to grasp the picture being presented on the radar and

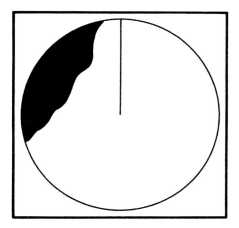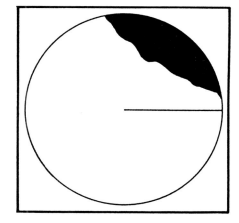

Head-up (left) and north-up displays showing the way the picture rotates to accommodate the different presentations. North-up displays require compass information and can be related directly to the chart – either paper or electronic.

relate it to what you see looking out of the windows of the wheelhouse. However, the north-up display is optional, so having this feature does enable you to get the picture that you think is right for the particular navigation circumstances in which you find yourself.

COLOUR RADAR

The standard radar display is monochrome, normally green or orange against a black background. In some cases it is possible to reverse this colour so that the background is orange or green and the targets and other features are black. However, the advent of high definition colour CRTs has led to the development of colour radar displays. On the surface this would appear to be a major step forward but in reality colour provides more of a pretty picture than a useful navigation aid, although the use of colour can make the display clearer in congested areas.

Colour can be used in different ways with a radar display. In the simplest form it is used as an extension of the monochrome display with the targets being shown in one colour against a contrasting background of another colour. It is often possible to vary the colour combination to give the optimum display for the ambient light conditions. On this type of display colour can be further employed with range rings or VRMs in a third colour, and where there is a facility for drawing lines on the display to indicate shallow water or traffic lanes these may be shown in yet another colour.

With this type of radar, colour is used solely to enhance the clarity of the display, each different feature using a different colour. This can be useful in making the display clearer for fast boat navigation, but other radars use colour in a more sophisticated manner which is related to the strength of the returned radar signal. In these displays red tends to be used for the strongest signals and green is usually reserved for the weakest, whilst in between there is a range of colours. Whilst it might appear logical to identify targets by the strength of their return in this way, in my experience it has little practical value. If colour has to be used in this way then I would much rather see the weak targets shown in red and the strong targets in green because in general the weaker targets will represent small craft or buoys and these need highlighting on the display. As they stand at present, the strong red returns shown on this type of display tend to dominate the screen, making it easier to miss the weak targets altogether.

In time a much more sophisticated use of colour will probably be employed in radar displays related more to the clear differentiation between different types of target, perhaps one colour being used for fixed targets and another for moving targets. This use of colour will greatly enhance this feature for fast boat operations, particularly in crowded waters when the radar screen can become saturated with targets. Any method which enables them to be readily identified must be beneficial.

For larger craft, this colour radar with its separate control panel makes an ideal installation, although the complex control panel could be improved to facilitate use. (Photo: Racal Marine.)

RADAR PERFORMANCE

What you see on the radar screen depends a great deal on the target. The radar beam emitted from the scanner tends to follow a straight line, but of course the earth is curved and so at some distance away only objects which appear over the horizon will reflect the radar pluse. This means that land some distance away may not be detected if it is low lying, or that you will just see the tops of hills and not the actual coastline. This can give a distorted picture on the radar display, particularly as you make a landfall, but of course as you approach the coastline the true picture will start to emerge. The type of material from which the target is constructed will also affect the radar return; metal and rock are the best reflectors. These are hard materials which absorb very little of the radar energy, reflecting most of it back. Softer surfaces such as sand or mud are poor reflectors, whilst vegetation, timber and fabrics reflect very little, which is one reason why radar does not pick up sailing boats very well despite their large size.

A vertical surface which is at right angles to the radar beam is also a good reflector which is why cliffs show up very well, whilst a sloping surface such as a beach will tend to dissipate the radar energy with less of the return being reflected to the scanner. A broken surface like a stony beach will be a good reflector because of the many angled surfaces which help to reflect the radar energy.

The returns from ships and boats will depend a great deal on their size. Large ships will probably be detectable on a small boat radar at ranges over 10 miles, whilst smaller ships may show up at between 5 and 10 miles. Buoys and small craft are not particularly good radar targets, while fibreglass and wooden yachts are amongst the worst; they may show up at only a couple of miles or so. When fitted with a radar reflector these detection ranges can double, but without a reflector small boats can easily be lost in the sea clutter which can extend up to two or three miles from your own vessel when the sea conditions are at all lively. Of course you should remember that other vessels may have the same problems with detecting your own craft, although fast boats tend to be good radar targets because the wake helps to strengthen the radar return. The wake can often be seen on the radar display extending astern as a tail, making the fast boat identifiable on the radar screen.

Navigation marks are not always good radar targets and buoys and lighthouses may not show up particularly well, although most major buoys today are fitted with a radar reflector which improves the situation. Light-vessels are better targets but again you have no way of identifying them from surrounding shipping except by the fact that they are stationary.

It is now becoming an increasingly common practice to fit important navigation marks with racons which are, in fact, radar transponders. When the radar signal hits the transponder it triggers a return signal which identifies the target by a series of large dots extending from the target out to the edge of the radar display. These racons are only fitted to certain important navigation marks because, if there are too many, you cannot distinguish one from the other and the picture becomes very confusing. They also tend to be activated only once every minute or so to prevent the display becoming saturated.

RADAR PROBLEMS

We have so far outlined the benefits of radar. Now it is time to consider the problems which can detract from its performance. It is important to understand this aspect because once you realise what the radar can't see then you can appreciate the limitations under which you are working.

Radar designers try to design the radar so that it will acquire targets under most conditions. The radar beam is about 25 degrees wide in the vertical plane which helps to allow for the rolling of the boat. In most cases this ensures that targets are not lost even though the boat may be rolling fairly heavily. With this wide beam angle you will find that the targets become weaker or even lost towards the edge of the beam if the boat rolls. Of course, if the beam goes below the horizon targets will be lost altogether, but this is a momentary loss and is nothing really to worry about because the target will probably be picked up on the next rotation of the scanner.

As far as the horizontal beam width is concerned the designers try to make this as narrow as possible so that the energy is concentrated to give maximum detection range. However, the horizontal beam width is largely determined by the length of the scanner. A short scanner of about two feet in length, typically found in small boats, will give a beam width of about 4 to 5 degrees, whereas a longer scanner up to four feet will narrow this down to perhaps 2 degrees. Whilst this may not seem to be a significant difference it can in fact have a considerable impact on the radar performance. With a beam width of 5 degrees any targets within this 5 degree sector will appear on the centre line of the beam as shown on the radar display. This means that if you have two targets separated by just under 5 degrees they would appear on the radar display as a single target. This can be confusing if there is a lot of shipping in the area as some craft will tend to merge. Perhaps more critical is that off-lying islands will tend to merge into the coastline as you approach them and features such as harbour entrances and narrow channels may not show up clearly. The one redeeming feature in all this is that as you get closer the two targets effectively move further apart in angle and eventually separate, so the picture will become clear, but there can be some anxious moments before this clarification occurs.

The wider beam width also dissipates the power over a wider area, reducing detection ranges. The moral, of course, is to buy the longest scanner you can afford and which you can accommodate on board, to get the best quality of radar pictures.

Much the same thing happens with the radar pulse being sent out. As we

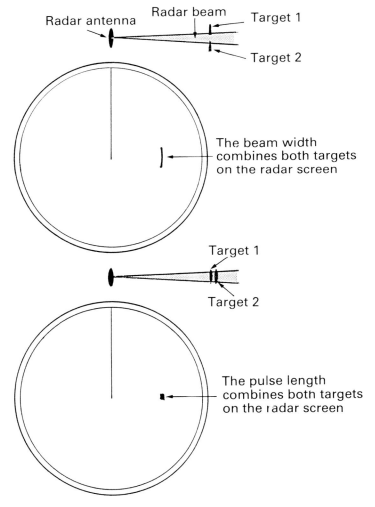

Top: A wide beam width on the radar will encompass two targets in the one beam and they will show up as a single elongated echo on the screen.
Bottom: Two targets on the same bearing can be encompassed by the same pulse so that they will show up as one.

have already seen, on the longer pulses these can extend for about 150 metres and so two vessels this distance apart will appear on the screen as a single target. In this situation the vessels will not separate as you approach unless, of course, you switch the range to one employing the shorter pulse length. This will then cause the individual vessels to separate out.

Sea clutter, the return received from waves in the vicinity of the vessel, is one of the features of radar which you could well do without but is one which is inherent in the system. In rough weather it could extend to four or five miles. Most small boat radars have a sea clutter control which enables you to reduce the gain in the area immediately around the vessel. This helps to clear the picture considerably, but you must bear in mind that the returns from the waves can be just as strong as those from small vessels, so by reducing the sensitivity you could cut out returns from small boat targets or buoys.

Some radars use more sophisticated processing techniques which only show radar returns which are received on perhaps four or five successive rotations of the scanner. The returns from sea clutter tend to be random so this processing helps to cut out many of the unwanted signals whilst retaining those from small vessels which are inside the sea clutter area. This type of processing does not solve the problem entirely, however, so you still need to take care that you are not losing small vessels when using such equipment.

The returns from sea clutter will always be worse from windward rather than from leeward. To windward the waves present a more vertical face towards the radar scanner thus giving a stronger return. This means that the sea clutter tends to follow a sort of oval shape around the centre of the radar display. One benefit of this is that you can at least tell the direction of the wind. Another feature which will be seen on the display is the return from your own wake which will tend to fan out from the stern of your vessel. Again you will be less interested in returns from astern, so this is not particularly critical.

Rain affects the radar and can return a considerable proportion of the transmitted pulses. These are shown on the screen as a large obliterated target area in which more important targets can be lost. Many radars have a rain control which helps to reduce the returns from rain targets, but in heavy showers or snow such a control certainly can't cut out the returns altogether. In these conditions you have to take great care in detecting approaching targets as actual visibility can also be considerably reduced.

Rain can be one of the worst situations you have to face in a fast boat when using radar. If you are at all unhappy about the situation then it is wise to reduce speed rather than plough on through heavy rain as it is so easy to lose important targets even when they are close to you.

RADAR EFFICIENCY

The efficiency of a radar should not be judged by its stated maximum range. Many small boat radars are offered with a range up to 48 miles, but there is no guarantee that you will pick up targets at this range. What is much more important is the transmitter power, and small boat radars with 3 kW transmitters will probably run out of steam at about 24 miles even with very strong targets: there will not be sufficient power to get a strong enough return at this range to activate the receiver. If you want longer ranges – and this can be useful when making landfalls – then you need a more powerful transmitter, perhaps 5 or 10 kW, but bear in mind that the size of the radar also increases and you may not have space for this on a small fast boat, quite apart from the additional weight factor which can be important.

The low sitting of the scanner on a fast boat will also reduce the chances of picking up targets at extreme ranges, and in my experience you are best using a maximum range of 12 miles. If on the other hand you are using the radar for collision avoidance, then the three mile range is one of the best to use.

A narrow channel like this one between an island and the mainland may not show up on a small boat radar until you are quite close, because of the wide horizontal beam angle.

Whilst considering transmission power and scanner sizes, do check that the radar scanner is capable of operating in very strong winds, say up to 100 knots, because you could find yourself travelling at 50 knots into quite a strong wind when you are close inshore in sheltered waters, and some radar scanners are not designed to cope with this. However, on most modern radars the scanner has been tested up to 100 knots which should be adequate for most practical purposes.

PARALLEL INDEXING

Parallel indexing is a technique used with radar which can be particularly useful on fast boats. On the earlier types of radar where the bearing cursor was a clear plastic disk placed over the top of the radar display and was operated mechanically, parallel indexing consisted of a series of lines engraved on the disk parallel to the heading marker and spaced at intervals corresponding with the range rings on the display. Since this type of mechanical bearing cursor faded from use, parallel indexing lines have also disappeared, although they are now making a reappearance on some more sophisticated radars and will no doubt eventually be found on most small boat radars because they can be useful.

The modern technique is to have the lines put on the screen electronically but as previously, they are still parallel to the heading marker and spaced at intervals corresponding to range rings, so that on the six mile range you will have 6 lines, each 1 mile apart. When the bearing cursor is rotated, so these parallel index lines also rotate and stay parallel.

We shall look more closely at how to use these features in Chapters 11 and 12, but basically these parallel index lines allow you to line up a target – whether it is land or another vessel ahead – and set a course to allow you to pass a fixed distance off that target. For instance, if you had a headland ahead and you wanted to pass one mile off it, then you could vary your course to line up with the parallel index line which is one mile off the heading marker along the headland, and then in theory the vessel follows along the heading marker whilst the headland will stay along the parallel index line. Using this technique

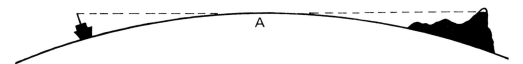

At longer ranges low targets may be below the radar horizon. Any targets beyond A will not show up unless they are high.

you can easily detect whether the vessel is moving in towards the headland or moving away from it, and in this way you can see where you are going to be ahead of time.

Much the same sort of technique can be used in collision avoidance, and on any fast boat radar these parallel index lines should be a feature to look for.

RADAR FOR NAVIGATION

As a navigation tool for fast boats radar is one of the most useful. It presents you with a picture of your surroundings in a plan view similar to that shown on a chart. Apart from setting up the radar properly and understanding its limitations, just two controls, the VRM and the VBM, tend to be used, and with these two you can carry out quite complex navigation with a degree of authority and flexibility which is not really possible with other systems. Electronic position-finding can help your navigation considerably provided you stay on set routes and courses, but with the radar you have a completely up-to-the-minute picture of the navigation situation. Provided you interpret the information correctly, you can navigate at high speed with a good measure of safety. It has the facility to maintain this ability at night and in poor visibility, although as we have seen in heavy rain you have to use a little more caution.

With radar it is possible to fix your position and transfer this to the chart, but in fast boat navigation this is not really practical. Indeed any position transferred to the chart in this way is likely to be only of historic interest because of the time lapse in transferring it, which can mean that you are a mile or more away from the position by the time you have marked it on the chart. If you do want to transfer a position onto the chart from radar then make range measurements with the VRM rather than bearings. The ranges will be very accurate whereas the bearings will only be as accurate as the compass heading which has to be applied to them.

A good fix from radar will use three ranges so that you have a check on them, and here it is important to make sure that you are taking the ranges from known features on the radar. It is very easy to make assumptions that a particular headland is the one you are looking for. You cannot be entirely sure because unfortunately the radar display does not have the names written on the headlands as you find on the chart. Instead, you have to identify the headland by its shape, and this is where the distortion sometimes found on the radar picture can lead you astray.

For fast boat navigation you will tend to use the radar as an extension of your eyeball navigation techniques, and this is where your parallel indexing comes in. If you are travelling along a coast you will want to pass a certain distance off the next headland, checking on the chart that the route is clear of offlying dangers. You can then line up the parallel index line and know that you will pass a safe distance around the headland provided that the headland is kept on or outside that index line. With eyeball navigation you do much the same sort of thing, setting the headland at an estimated distance off the bow and following along that track; with radar you can keep the distance off much more precisely. Even without parallel index lines you can still judge the distance off as you would with eyeball navigation, only you can't be quite so precise.

On a fast boat it is best to use the land as a reference for navigation as far as possible because this is easy to identify in most cases. Lightvessels, buoys and isolated lighthouses can also be used provided you can make a positive identification. Here, of course, the racon can be invaluable to pick out, say, a lightship in crowded waters. This enables you to set a course direct for this mark or just clear of it as the case may be. Lighthouses tend to be placed either just off the land or on the land so that you can identify them on the radar in relation to the other land features, but isolated lighthouses will invariably have a racon, so you should be able to pick these out as well. Buoys are a different matter and isolated buoys can be quite difficult to identify. Buoys marking a channel can often be identified on the screen because of the particular pattern they adopt, but you need to be a little cautious here until you can make a positive sighting or identification.

Sandbanks may only show up on the radar display at close range and here it is often the broken water around the edge which returns the strongest echo and gives you a positive identification. Isolated rocks should show up clearly, but bear in mind the problems already mentioned with the wide horizontal radar beam which can make these rocks merge together or into the land, so that they may not always be readily identifiable some distance away.

In clear weather in daylight radar can serve as a useful check to your eyeball navigation which should be able to cope with the situation without too much assistance. Using the radar in this way, apart from being a check, also gives you good practice at using the radar, which can be invaluable when you are faced with the more serious problems of navigating at night or in fog. Another use of the radar in clear weather is to gain practice at judging distances which can enhance the reliability of your eyeball navigation. A little practice at distance judging and then confirming or otherwise by what is seen on the radar can give you confidence in your ability to judge distances reliably.

Radar can be particularly valuable in daytime on approaching a harbour, when it is not always easy to pick out the harbour entrance against the land in the background. Because the radar shows a plan view, the piers or jetties will often show up quite clearly on the radar separated from the background land, and this can give you a useful guide to your way into harbour until visual techniques can take over.

At night time radar can become particularly valuable in this way because harbour lights can often be lost against the confused background lighting. Likewise, the lights of other vessels using or entering the harbour may be hard to distinguish, though these will show up quite clearly on the radar.

In clear weather, whether by day or by night, the role of radar in fast boat navigation is really one of confirmation and help by the provision of additional information. You could cope without the radar, but it is nice to have that extra reassurance and assistance. When it comes to poor visibility then radar assumes great importance for navigation. With electronic position-finding

The digital information on this small radar may be hard to read at high speed, but with a remote control panel the radar meets most of the requirements for fast navigation. (Photo: Vigil Radar.)

you will be able to maintain course and speed, but because you are travelling virtually blind you have to put a great deal of faith in the electronics. With radar you can obtain a picture of what is going on around you in poor visibility which can be tremendously reassuring – but as always with radar, don't take too much for granted. To use radar successfully for fast boat navigation you need to concentrate on the display. At the speeds at which you are travelling it is very easy to lose track of the features along a coastline unless you identify each one as it comes up and mentally or physically mark it off on the chart. In this way you will keep track of progress and know where you are in relation to the coastline shown on the radar screen, always remembering that the features of the coastline will not always look exactly the same as they are shown on the chart.

Radar can be particularly valuable when making a landfall, and indeed when switched to its extreme range can give you the first indication of land even before it looms up over the horizon. You can't read too much into the information given at these distances but it is nice to know that the land is there, and as you approach the coast features will start to emerge much more clearly on the screen. However, it is very easy to make the features which you see on the screen fit what you expect to see. You may try to convince yourself that the headland shown on the radar screen has the same shape as the headland you want to find as shown on the chart, and persuade yourself that the slight difference in shape is caused by the distortion of the radar picture, when in fact it could be a different headland altogether if you are some way off course. This is one good reason why you also need to look for clearly identifiable features along the coastline when making a landfall. These features should be identifiable both by the naked eye and on the radar by their unique shapes.

Navigating successfully with radar requires considerable practice in order to build up confidence, particularly when it comes to operating at high speeds. Fine weather practice will give you the confidence to rely on equipment in poor visibility and this can be even more important when it comes to collision avoidance. Concentration is also vital, particularly in poor visibility, so it's a good idea to have one crew member dedicated to watching the radar screen.

6 Compass, log and dead reckoning

Pointing the boat in the right direction is one of the basic essentials of navigation. In a fast boat it is important to get an accurate heading, but the conditions on a fast boat can make it difficult for a compass to operate effectively. In many fast boats, particularly on racing boats, there is a somewhat casual approach to the compass, and yet if you go off course you could travel a considerable distance without realising the mistake. Compasses can be made to operate in this difficult environment, but like most things in fast boats, it does require attention to detail (see below).

Getting a log to work in the fast boat environment is equally difficult. There is no really workable solution at present and the few speed logs on the market are probably only accurate at best to 10 per cent. At speeds of 80 mph this can result in considerable errors if you are trying to navigate by dead reckoning. When you combine the problems of compass and log, then dead reckoning becomes a less than accurate art on fast boats, but if you are aware of the inaccuracies you can make allowances for them.

MAGNETIC COMPASS

Install the normal magnetic compass in a boat which is tossing around at sea and the card will swing all over the place. This swing is partly due to the heeling error, which induces temporary errors in the compass when the boat heels over, but it is mainly caused by the heavy shock loadings on the compass which tend to accelerate any momentum in the swinging compass card. Trying to site the compass on some type of shock absorbing mount doesn't help the problem; if anything, it makes it worse because the whole compass can then move slightly under the shock loadings. Nor is it possible to damp out the wide variety of vibration frequencies.

For fast boat use, the solution adopted by most compass manufacturers is to increase the viscosity of the damping oil inside the compass. The thicker oil reduces any sudden motion of the compass card, and vanes fitted to the card itself also help. The problem is finding the delicate balance between adequate damping to reduce the swinging and too much damping which will reduce the sensitivity of the compass. The compass card needs to be kept as light as possible to reduce the inertia, which means that only small light magnets can be used which reduces the directional stability of the card. With limited stability, only limited damping can be accommodated.

Modern fast boat compasses are remarkably good considering the inherent compromises which the designers have to make. In most conditions they provide reasonably reliable heading information, but they do require user input in the form of averaging out the movements of the compass card to steer the mean course. This means that the helmsman has to spend more time looking at the compass than at the sea ahead.

A modern electronic compass with a clear, easy-to-read dial. At high speeds, all displays need to be easily readable because of the movement of the boat.

ELECTRONIC COMPASS

The electronic or fluxgate compass suffers from no such damping problems because this can be achieved electronically. This does not affect the direction seeking qualities of the instrument which are consistent, but the readings of the compass can be averaged electronically both in terms of time and deviation from the mean heading, so that the work is done for the helmsman and he can be presented with a steady heading reference. Some compasses allow the electronic damping to be controlled but this must not be overdone otherwise the compass will not respond readily to changes of heading which can be quite rapid on a fast boat. Different conditions also require different damping levels, so not all fluxgate compasses are suitable for fast boats. Check in the handbook to see if the compass has variable damping which you can control. If so, increase the damping to the point where the compass becomes sluggish on a right turn. This is too much damping so you will need to reduce it a little from this point.

Fluxgate compasses are susceptible to heeling error caused when the boat heels, and as the sensing coils have to be suspended their inertia can also make them swing under the violent movement of the boat. When the compass swings in this way the sensing power of the coils is reduced and this characteristic can be used to bias the electronic damping in favour of the readings taken when the coils are horizontal and to ignore them when the boat is heeled. A refinement of this is to incorporate a rate gyro into the system which can help to maintain short-term stability in the compass readings when the fluxgate compass readings are erratic. Manufacturers are developing a combined fluxgate/gyro system which could be the way ahead for future fast boat compasses.

Excessive damping on either a fluxgate or a standard magnetic compass can cause the compass to lag behind the boat's head on a turn. For cruising this is unlikely to be much of a problem, but when racing you can have difficulty setting a new course after a sharp turn unless the rate of turn is slowed to allow the compass to catch up. With the compass lagging behind on the turn, the boat will overshoot the turn if you are relying on it to indicate the new course. This is why you often see race boats steering a wiggle when they come out of a tight turn; they are trying to cope with a compass which takes time to catch up.

There are two types of fluxgate compass, both of which use sensitive coils to detect the earth's magnetic field. A single coil will pick up the strongest signal when it is in line with the earth's magnetic field. With this type the navigator has to set his required course on a dial, and the compass indicator is a simple left/right instrument showing the way to steer to bring the vessel back on course. For a fast boat such an indicator can be easy to steer to because a quick glance will show what to steer — there are no numbers to read and interpret and no course to remember. It allows you to concentrate more on the sea ahead.

However, tradition still has a strong influence on compass design and the majority of fluxgate compasses use a double coil sensor which allows the compass information to be displayed in a conventional manner with a 360° compass card. One of the benefits of this type of fluxgate compass is that because the output is electronic, it can be fed into alternative types of display to suit the application. The same can be done with the normal magnetic compass when sensor coils are fitted, but the resulting complication is not really justified when fluxgate compasses are available.

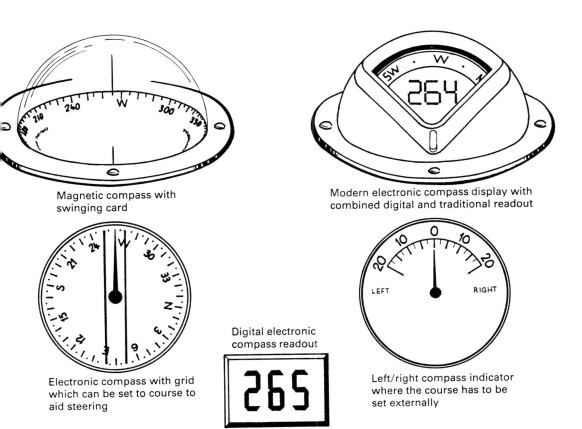

Magnetic compass with swinging card

Modern electronic compass display with combined digital and traditional readout

Electronic compass with grid which can be set to course to aid steering

Digital electronic compass readout

Left/right compass indicator where the course has to be set externally

Alternative compass displays for high speed craft.

COMPASS DISPLAYS

For steering a fast boat the prime requirement is clear unambiguous heading information. This is why the left/right indicator is good, but it does require practice to get used to it and most fast boats settle for a more traditional approach. When a magnetic compass is used, the compass card has to be horizontal, but the dished type of card makes reading easier when the compass is in the best position, a little below eye level. With a compass card embracing a full circle there are limitations on its size, and this in turn limits the size of figures and lines on the card. This can cause difficulties in reading the card at speed, particularly when it is mounted in the optimum position, some distance in front of the helmsman so that he doesn't need to change his eye focus too much. Much the same applies to the fully circular compass dials used for fluxgate compasses, but these dials do have the advantage of being capable of being mounted at any angle.

One way of improving the readability of a compass is to use a grid. This is a pair of double parallel lines engraved on a cursor which can be rotated over the compass dial. The grid is set to the required course so that steering is then simply a matter of keeping the north line on the rotating dial between the two parallel lines. This system is good for fluxgate compass dials which can be mounted at or near the vertical but a magnetic compass has to be mounted lower so that you can look down into it, which is far from ideal in a fast boat.

Digital displays where the boat's heading is shown simply in numbers are gaining popularity. I am surprised at how easy it is to steer an accurate course with such a display, and modern digital displays have good sized figures to make reading easy. You still have to remember the course you are steering but as they are often combined with a left/right signal this gives you an indication of when you are on the correct course. One of the benefits of the fluxgate compass is that the display can be tailored to match closely the specific requirements of different types of craft. However, the particular requirements of fast boats may be swallowed up in the manufacturers' desire to cover as large a sector of the market as possible.

COMPASS CORRECTIONS

Magnetic compasses whether standard or fluxgate are subject to errors: variation from the difference between true and magnetic north, and deviation from the influence of the boat's own magnetic field. Variation is more or less fixed for a particular geographical area and does not change with heading, so it is fairly easy to cope with. It is simply a question of applying a fixed correction to the magnetic or the true heading to convert one to the other. On many fluxgate compasses it is possible to correct for the variation so that it is applied automatically.

Deviation is much more complex. Not only does it vary with heading, but it can also vary with time. Deviation is found by a compass adjuster 'swinging' the boat; having done so one or two magnets are then fitted around the compass largely to cancel out the influence of the boat's magnetic field and reduce the deviation to one or two degrees on most headings. This can only be done if there are no major magnetic influences close to the compass, which emphasises the need to plan the wheelhouse layout carefully.

In this way deviation can be coped with and, if it is only a degree or two, can be ignored on short runs. The problem arises from the way in which deviation can change with time. This is due to the pounding of the boat at sea which can change the boat's magnetic influence, though you can suffer the same effect if the boat has been trailed by road for some distance. It can be an expensive business calling out the compass adjuster at regular intervals, so an alternative is to check the compass yourself to see if there has been any change.

I would advocate regular checking of the compass on a fast boat. This applies to both the normal type of magnetic compass and the fluxgate type because they are both equally affected. It is also a good idea to check the compass before doing a long run over open water to confirm that the compass is giving accurate heading information or to ascertain the error you have to apply.

There are two ways of checking. One is to look at the chart and find transit bearings to use. These should be fixed objects rather than buoys which can move away from their assigned position. It is not always easy to find transits on the particular heading you want to check, so a useful alternative is to use a hand bearing compass. If you stand up on deck away from the superstructure and the engines you will be clear of their magnetic influence. Line up the hand bearing compass with a point on the shore and then line up the boat with the same point. If you compare the readings of the two compasses you will either confirm that the steering compass is giving the correct reading or find the error as the difference between the two, the hand bearing compass reading being taken as the correct one. You will still have to apply variation. When doing this ensure that you have no magnetic materials in your pocket.

Do remember that a check is simply that – a check and not a substitute for the compass adjuster. Any corrections found necessary will only apply to that particular heading, and you may want to check out several headings before setting off.

Remember to take care over compass correction. On some fluxgate equipment the variation is applied automatically. In some cases you can feed in the deviation as well so that this is also applied automatically. This can allow you to work with true courses but be careful to check that *all* the courses you use are corrected. Some equipment may be corrected and some not, so confusion can arise.

GYRO COMPASSES

The gyro compass is an expensive piece of equipment but it does have the benefit of indicating true north, so you have no worries with variation and deviation. Cost and size will tend to rule out gyro compasses for smaller boats, but on any craft over, say, 75 feet in length they are worth considering. They offer a stable and reliable heading indication, and in my experience can cope with the motion of fast boats despite the delicate nature of their internal machinery.

COMPASS OUTPUTS

With modern electronics, the compass is just one of many sensors which build up the navigation picture. Apart from providing heading information for steering, the compass can be required to interface with the radar and possibly the electronic chart. If you have a Transit satellite navigator this requires either manual or automatic compass input. The other major user of heading information is the autopilot.

There are usually few problems in taking outputs from fluxgate and gyro compasses, but remember that different compasses give different types of output and you should ensure that the signals are compatible. Some of the simple types of fluxgate compass are self-contained and do not have any facility for outputs to other equipment or even repeaters. With a standard magnetic compass, some of the more expensive versions can be or are fitted with sensor coils which translate the card heading into electrical signals for connecting to other equipment.

ALTERNATIVE HEADING INFORMATION

Your electronic position-fixing equipment will tell you the course and distance you are making good, but this is historical information and cannot be used for steering as such, although it can be used for correcting the course. The course information presented in this way has been averaged over a period of time to avoid the wild fluctuations which might occur if it was taken between every fix of the receiver. It should be remembered that this course made good information is the course over the ground and not through the water, the difference being the tide or the current.

There may come a time in the future when position-fixing receivers will provide heading information that one can steer to. If you had two receivers with one antenna in the bow and one at the stern, then by an electronic comparison of the two readings, you could obtain heading information. Such a heading system is feasible using the high accuracy GPS satellite system and would not be dependent on the absolute accuracy of the GPS positions since both receivers would be equally affected by errors. It is doubtful whether such a system would be viable on smaller craft because of the short base line of the measurement, but it could be a possibility for vessels over 100 feet in length.

AUTOPILOTS

There is no doubt in my mind that steering with an autopilot is much more efficient than manual steering provided it does its job. The autopilot doesn't get tired or lose its concentration, and keeps to the course whatever the distractions outside. Autopilots have a role in fast boats, but there can be difficulties in getting an autopilot to work efficiently. The problems can be a combination of steering, which is very sensitive, a boat which responds quickly to wave influence, and a worry that the autopilot might react adversely to a transient change in wave patterns.

I have used autopilots in boats travelling at up to 50 knots, and there can be problems with the autopilot response which are associated with the drive system. Rudders have a comparatively low steering response whilst drives which incorporate steering, such as stern drives and water jets, have a strong steering response which the autopilot can have difficulty in coping with. A slight adjustment can produce a strong steering response with the result that the course is over-corrected. In this situation the boat tends to progress in a series of sweeps rather than on a straight course. On most autopilots it is possible to adjust the sensitivity to improve this, but I have found that you can run out of adjustment before the problem is solved.

Within the limits of current autopilot technology the autopilot will lose control if the boat becomes or is close to becoming airborne. In this situation the autopilot can send a message to the steering which duly responds. Without a corresponding response in the heading a larger angle of steering is commanded. The boat then re-enters with the steering off centre which could cause the boat to spin out of control, at least temporarily. Therefore in any situation in which the boat is close to becoming airborne the autopilot should not be used.

A combined autopilot and plotter with interface between the two. A position fixing receiver needs to be linked in to give position information, and then you have an integrated system which gives the ability to navigate with confidence at high speeds. (Photo: Cetrek Ltd.)

Obviously in smaller craft this situation will be reached earlier than in larger craft, so the speed at which autopilots can be used is a function of the sea conditions and the size of the vessel. However, this is certainly a case where you need to err on the side of safety and watch out for the wash of passing ships which could create waves larger than the average.

In general, then, autopilots should be used with caution in fast boats, although with rudder steering you will be much safer. The advantages of using the autopilot are that you will follow a much straighter course which will help the dead reckoning. It will remove helmsman's bias, but check that the autopilot doesn't have its own bias, steering to one side perhaps to counter a beam wind or locking on to one side of the dead band. In fog or other conditions where the radar is vital, the straight course steered by the autopilot can help stabilise the radar picture. Finally the autopilot can release the helmsman from concentrating on the steering and is a very useful ally in a one-man wheelhouse.

The autopilot will only be as good as its compass sensor, and some of the compasses supplied with autopilots are not damped adequately for high speed work. In most cases you can use an alternative compass, and you may have to experiment a little to get things right. Some autopilots can also introduce a form of damping to smooth out the swinging of the compass, so you will need to get to know the controls of your autopilot and how they work. It is also possible to link a position-fixing receiver to the autopilot, and with cross track error information it is possible for the autopilot to maintain the vessel on a prescribed track rather than a prescribed course.

LOGS

Getting a log to work efficiently on a fast boat is also very difficult. All logs rely on a transducer in the water to provide the raw information about speed which, when it is processed, allows the speed and distance to be displayed in the wheelhouse. The transducer needs a clean, solid water flow in order to give reliable readings, and such a water flow can be hard to find on a fast boat. The problems get worse on smaller craft and when operating in waves when there is a greater chance of the boat becoming airborne.

There are various types of log, the difference being largely in the transducer which is used. Paddle wheel and impeller type logs are generally adequate up to 30–40 knots provided there is a good water flow, whilst the electromagnetic and the Sonic logs which have no moving parts under water can usually work up to 40–50 knots. Over 50 knots the pitot tube log is best, which measures the pressure of the water in a small tube positioned in the water flow past the hull. These logs can work up to 100 knots or more, and are best for high speed work becoming more sensitive as higher speeds are reached, but they are very insensitive at speeds below 50 knots. These logs still need a good water flow, and on race boats the sensor is positioned on the bottom of the rudder or the engine drive leg to keep it as low as possible.

Where logs produce electronic signals, these can be processed to give a form of damping which will produce more consistent readings; on some units the damping or averaging can be adjusted to suit requirements. This has to be done with care if you are using the distance run for dead reckoning.

Another source of speed information can come from electronic position-fixing equipment, but as with the course taken from this source, it is speed over the ground and not speed through the water which is given. When there is full coverage by GPS the speeds obtained will be more consistent because of the better accuracy of the positions given.

It would be nice to have a good speed indicator on a fast boat to use for tuning and perhaps to assess the merits of different sizes of propeller, but none of the logs currently available is suitable except for speeds up to the 30–40 knot range. For tuning you will use relative speeds, but for navigation work you are interested in the absolute speed, and for this the log will need calibrating whatever type it is. Calibrating means running the boat over a measured distance and comparing the speed shown with that measured. Some logs can be adjusted so that they show the true speed, but the errors can vary over the speed range. Any calibration should be done when there is little or no wind, and runs in both directions are necessary to even out the effect of tides or currents.

DEAD RECKONING

Dead reckoning seems to be living up to its name and becoming a dying art. Modern electronics provide the navigator with accurate positions almost on demand, so why take the trouble to keep a detailed plot of courses and speeds? In fast boats such a pilot is almost impossible anyway as we have seen, but with eyeball navigation you *are* carrying out a form of mental dead reckoning so that you have a fair idea of where you are. However, the bulk of the work should already have been done in your preparation.

In slower, comfortable boats dead reckoning means keeping a more or less continuous plot because you will be much more sensitive to tides and winds. In a fast boat you have committed yourself to a course and all you can really do along the way is make a mental note or write down the times you pass any significant navigational point. In this way you will have a reference point to work out your dead reckoning from if things go wrong, perhaps if you lose an engine or fog comes down. You will not then be completely lost.

With electronic navigation you should use much the same technique. Whilst the electronics are working satisfactorily you have no problems; you have up-to-date positions at your fingertips. But what do you do if the screen suddenly goes blank? If you have jotted down your position and time at regular intervals then you are not lost. All you have to do is take the last position, apply your course and speed, and tides if necessary, and you can quickly arrive at a good estimate of your current position. From there you can plot the course to where you want to go. To do this you will probably have to come off the plane, but that's a small price to pay for coping with an electronic failure.

The biggest problem with this technique is laziness. You may go year after year without a failure of your electronics and it is easy to get bored with noting the position at regular intervals. When the failure finally occurs you may have given up writing down the positions altogether. The problem you will face is the result of slack navigation techniques. Just as you must do a considerable amount of preparation work which you may not use, so you must also do work on passage which you might not use. The problem is that you never know when the situation will change until it does. If you want to be a competent navigator then you must be able to cope with the unexpected. Take the easy approach if you want to, but be prepared to face the consequences if you do. Dead reckoning is far from dead as far as fast boats are concerned, but you can simplify the techniques.

7 Wheelhouse design

In the fast boat environment conditions are far from ideal for concentrating on driving and navigating the boat. However, a great deal can be done to improve the situation by careful design and layout of the wheelhouse or steering position. This is something of a grey area, with the designer tending to draw up a basic layout which could well have more to do with aesthetics than practical requirements. The detailed layout is generally left to the boatyard to sort out and they will tend to position equipment where it is convenient rather than practical. On production boats the layout may be worked out in more detail, but then such boats rarely have more than very basic electronics as standard, so any additions the owner wants to make have to be fitted around the existing layout, which can be far from ideal.

This situation has developed largely from the almost total absence of standardisation, so the navigator and the driver are faced with a hotchpotch of dials, displays and controls, none of them in the optimum position and none of them capable of being used to their full potential as a result. There is really only one way to get things right, and that is to build a mock-up of the wheelhouse so that the layout can be planned in three dimensions. Even then you need understanding of the various requirements and considerable experience because in the limited space available there will still be many compromises which have to be made.

On craft such as patrol boats, pilot boats and other commercial vessels where long hours can be spent in the wheelhouse, there is likely to be a more receptive attitude towards getting things right. However, this is often accompanied by a conservative or traditional viewpoint which tends to want to do things the way they have always been done, without realising that the speed of the craft may be much higher than previous experience allows for, and that things have to change to meet the new demands. On pleasure craft the wheelhouse or control area often has to double up as a social area in harbour, and as the craft will usually spend much more time in harbour than at sea the social requirements may have priority over those of practical navigation.

At the end of the day you will only be able to drive and navigate the boat as well as the controls and instruments allow. You may not be able to realise the full potential of a good boat with a high speed capability simply because the wheelhouse layout is not adequate for the job. In general, as the speed rises so there is a greater need to concentrate on the driving and navigating layout; the best arrangements are seen in offshore racing boats where high speed is the overwhelming priority. These craft show just what can be achieved, but even on slower craft there is no reason why good layouts cannot be matched to the other requirements if they are considered at an early stage in the design. Here we will look at these various requirements and consider how they can be co-ordinated.

GENERAL LAYOUT

One of the first decisions to make about wheelhouse layout is the number and duties of the crew who will run the boat. In a patrol boat there could be well defined positions such as skipper, helmsman and navigator, but other commercial and pleasure craft would generally operate on a much looser arrangement which would depend on the circumstances. Offshore racing boats demonstrate the most dedicated approach to particular roles with a three-person crew comprising helmsman (pilot), navigator and throttleman. There is no doubt that this is the optimum arrangement for a boat travelling at very high speeds as it allows each person to concentrate on the particular job they have to do.

In some racing boats the crew has been reduced to two, either giving the job of navigator to the helmsman or splitting it between the two. This is putting real pressure on the crew because of the extra workload, and it is not uncommon to see such boats making navigational errors simply through lack of concentration, or resorting to following one of the other boats because that greatly reduces the navigation workload.

Away from the pressures of racing, a two-person crew working the boat is very reliable, and the best division is probably to have one on wheel and throttles and the other doing the navigation. On the throttles you need a close view of the waves to read them and adjust the throttles accordingly, whilst on the wheel you need to be able to read the compass – two viewpoints which do not conflict too greatly in distance. The navigator, on the other hand, has more freedom in terms of time and can vary his concentration from scanning the horizon for visual clues or approaching vessels to studying the output from the electronic instrumentation.

A two-station wheelhouse designed for this type of operation is relatively easy to develop, and provided there are always two people to operate the boat it's fine. However, many such boats will operate much of the time with just one person in the wheelhouse, usually in good visibility, in calm or moderate seas, or maybe because there is only one experienced person on board. Now the problems start because you will need the two-station layout in fog, at night in crowded waters, or at any time when there is pressure on the navigation, yet this two-station layout has also to be capable of being operated by just one person in less demanding situations.

If this is going to be achieved in a practical manner, then the two stations need to be side by side so that the instruments and controls are close together. This gives the helmsman a chance to see the electronic screens when required, but there is always the danger that he will tend to concentrate on these because they can present a more interesting view than that outside where he *should* be concentrating. This is particularly the case at night. If there is always to be a two-person crew operating the boat then it is much better to separate the two stations physically so that the navigation station does not

An integrated navigation area which makes the navigator's job easy. Facing the navigator are radar and chart plotter whilst position fixing receivers are at the side. This was the system used on *Azimut Atlantic Challenger.*

become a distraction for the helmsman. Placing the navigation area slightly behind the helm can be a good way of achieving this physical separation.

On fast pleasure boats the social aspect also has to be considered, and the double side-by-side station can be a good way of achieving this. Where boats are used just on short day-trips in familar waters, then there is less need for a formal separation of the work stations, but a provision for laying out a folded chart securely should be incorporated so that the mental checking of the navigation can be related quickly to what is shown on the chart.

SEATING

One of the biggest problems on many fast boats is that you have to use both hands to hold on with simply because the seating is inadequate. Although seating is preferable, a standing position is acceptable as used in many racing boats, provided in both cases that the occupant has adequate support and can have at least one hand free for pressing buttons on the electronics or working the throttles. The steering wheel is designed for steering the boat and if you have to use it as a handhold rather than a steering wheel then the seating or supports are not doing their job. If the helmsman is working both wheel and throttles then two hands are needed for the job and the seating becomes even more important. Similarly with the navigator, because he or she can only do a reasonable job if secure in the boat and not holding on for grim death.

It's not just being able to do a job of work which becomes a practical proposition when you have adequate seating; there is a lot of pleasure to be gained from fast travel on the water, but there is little enjoyment when you have to hang on tightly with both hands against the movement of the boat.

The design of good seating needs careful consideration. The padding should be firm rather than soft because you want it to absorb the hard rather than the gentle shocks. A two tier padding, soft on the outside and firm on the inside is a good compromise. The seat should give good support particularly around the hips and the shoulders because there is often quite violent sideways movement on a fast boat, and this sort of support helps to hold you securely. Finally a head rest with sideways support is useful on long trips because your neck muscles can get very tired.

A compromise seat design is appearing on some fast boats which has a fold-away squab. With the squab down you have a standing position with the wrap around back providing excellent support. With the squab in the raised position you have a comfortable seat. These seats tend to have a low back which makes them unsuitable for seat belts. I favour a raised back and seat belts because then you are held firmly in the seat and you can relax knowing that you will be held in place whatever the boat does and you can concentrate on the job in hand. Seat belts should be of the full harness type; two shoulder straps linking into a lap strap. The straps need to be well padded to prevent chafe with the movement of the boat.

CONTROLS

Although not strictly part of the navigation scene, the controls are important because they take priority over everything else in the layout of the dashboard. There are four controls which have to be considered: the steering wheel and the throttles/gears as the primary controls, and then the optional flaps and power trim controls which may or may not be present. A further control found on some fast boats is for filling and emptying the bow ballast tank.

The favoured position for the steering wheel is vertical in front of the driver. This is reasonable when standing, but when sitting it can be impossible to get your knees under the wheel and so you sit in an uncomfortable position. Also it is not easy to get good leverage on a vertical wheel particularly when you are steering with only one hand as is often the case. I think we can take a lesson here from truck drivers who have a steering wheel tilted 20–30 degrees from the horizontal. This gives a much more positive feeling of control in a fast boat and can be used in both the standing and sitting positions. You can get your

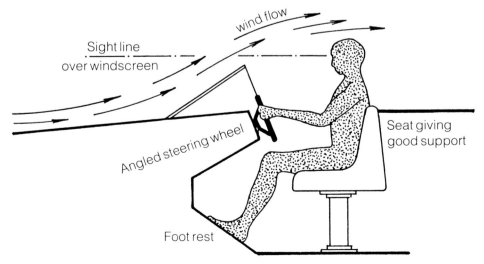

Points to look for in an open steering position. Supported in this way, the driver will be able to pay full attention to controlling the boat.

knees well underneath the wheel and with a well angled foot rest you are in a good position to steer the boat properly.

In so many fast boats I have tested the throttles have been badly placed. These are the controls that need constant use when a boat is being driven hard, and careful attention to the positioning can do a great deal to increase the rapport between the driver and the boat. In a two-station layout, the throttles need to be on the side away from the second station, and the almost universal standard is to have the steering position offset to starboard with the throttles on the right-hand side. Here the navigator or passenger will not interfere with the free movement of the throttles.

In order to use the throttles properly the throttle hand/arm needs to be located in relation to the boat, otherwise it will be subject to involuntary movement as the boat moves. You want delicate throttle control and so an arm/elbow rest suitably padded should be built in behind the throttle levers. The levers themselves should be angled so that the section of movement relating to top speeds is somewhere near the vertical position so that this will have the most sensitive control. At slow speeds the movement of the boat will be much less violent and so it is easier to cope with the throttle lever position.

You will notice that I haven't mentioned gears in this discourse, and this is because I am a firm believer in separating gear and throttle controls on fast boats. At sea you want only the throttles, whilst in harbour manoeuvring you virtually use only the gears. Separating them can give much greater sensitivity for the throttle opening, and there is no risk of bringing the lever right back and taking the propeller out of gear. The gear levers should be placed where they can't be knocked accidentally at sea, which probably means outboard of the throttle levers or even on the opposite side of the wheel.

With throttles and steering wheel you will have your hands full controlling the boat. If the flap and power trim controls are added, then you really need to be something of an octopus to cope. Power trim controls are often incorporated into the throttle levers, although with twin levers it can be difficult to operate twin switches. If not on the levers then the switches should be located where they can be easily reached and operated with one hand. In most cases you want to operate both flaps or both power trims together, so it helps if the two switches are combined, with separate switches for individual control when needed.

INSTRUMENTATION

Here we are talking about instruments such as the log, compass, echo sounder and engine instrumentation. The common feature of all these is that they provide information without the need for any interaction on the part of the user, and traditionally they are the instruments which are put in front of the helmsman. To a large degree they are monitoring instruments, showing the state of health of the boat and its progress, and providing the information which allows the helmsman to keep an eye on what is going on. It's worth looking at the role of these instruments more closely because, whilst they provide useful information, they can also serve as a distraction to the helmsman from his primary job of watching the waves ahead. This distraction is more severe at night when there is not much to see outside and these instruments provide something which is easy to focus on.

There is no arguing about the role of the compass. From time immemorial it has provided the vital heading information which serves to keep the boat on course when there may be little other indication. You can steer on visual landmarks or even by looking at the radar but the compass is always there when the others cannot provide information. The position of the compass is directly in front of the helmsman, but careful siting can both improve its performance and facilitate its use.

We have already seen how the compass should be kept away from other magnetic influence, and most of these will be the electronic and electrical instruments. This requirement combines with the need to mount the compass a good distance ahead of the helmsman – not so far that he can't read it, but far enough so that he doesn't have to change the focus of his eyes too much when glancing from the compass to the waves and back again. The level of the compass should be below the level line of sight, but only so that the line of sight changes slightly when glancing at the compass. In many wheelhouses the position of the windscreen will limit the position of the compass internally but don't dismiss the idea of mounting the compass outside.

A flat surface is required for a standard swinging card magnetic compass, but with fluxgate or gyro compasses there is a lot more flexibility in where the repeaters can be mounted. They are smaller and can be mounted at any angle, so there is a chance here to try a variety of alternative positions. However, the same basic principles apply of keeping the compass as close to the line of sight as possible.

The log and echo sounder are way down the list of priorities as far as positioning is concerned. Both are useful to the navigator as well as the helmsman, perhaps the echo sounder more so. Most echo sounders tend to become erratic at high speed so will only be of value when navigating at lower speeds, though it can be particularly valuable when entering harbour or narrow channels. It should be placed somewhere where it is easily visible but not at the expense of more important instruments. The log can be valuable to the helmsman when adjusting the power trim, and whilst it is nice to know the speed, again the priority of the display position is not high.

Tradition has it that engine monitoring instruments should occupy the prime space on the dashboard in front of the helmsman. When engines were less than reliable and there was little competition from other instruments there was logic in this location. Today engine monitoring instruments are much lower on the list of priorities, partly because engines are generally very reliable with regard to the parameters being monitored and partly because audio or visual alarms are generally connected to alert you to any problems. The chance that you will actually be looking at the instruments when a fault occurs is small, and it is much better to rely on the alarms and then look at the instruments to identify the problem. However, don't put the engine instruments too far away because a glance can be very reassuring and you can detect faults beginning by a small change in one of the readings. One of the best positions is in an overhead panel above the windscreen in an enclosed wheelhouse or off to one side in an open cockpit. Here the instruments can be easily seen without creating a distraction from the primary displays.

The exceptions here are the rev counters. I like to have these in front of me because they tell you a great deal about what is going on. Once you get to know

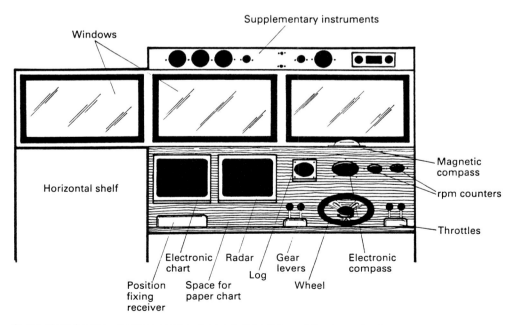

Some ideas for the wheelhouse layout on a fast boat to put the important instruments in the right place.

them, they give you an indication of speed, they can indicate problems, and they show immediately which is the troublesome one if one engine stops – something which can happen when manoeuvring in harbour or if you pick up a rope or debris at sea.

So the rev counters and the compass are all that the helmsman really needs in front of him. He requires easy access to switches such as the engine start/stop switches and those for the windscreen wipers and perhaps some of the lights. The aim should be to reduce distraction as much as possible, but to have other information like engine monitoring and navigation information close at hand when required. In this way the helmsman can concentrate on the primary job in hand, but can fulfil other functions if he finds himself single-handed.

NAVIGATION REQUIREMENTS

For navigation the paper chart is of primary importance even if an electronic chart system is planned. There will never be room to lay out a paper chart to its full extent in the limited space around the steering/navigation area, although it is useful to have somewhere on board where this is possible in order to do your preparatory work before leaving harbour. For use at sea the chart can be folded or cut up into a manageable size, and with an inside wheelhouse you can simply hold it in your hand when you need to study it and stow it away when not in use. With open steering positions the wind and water will soon destroy the chart if you have it loose in this way. The best solution is a place to lay out the chart under a clear plastic cover. This will give it protection and prevent wind blowing it overboard – but you do lose some of the chart clarity, which is another good reason to highlight the features of particular interest before setting off.

Even if using a folded chart, a chart table takes up considerable space, which may be at a premium if you want to install electronic equipment. Of the electronics, the radar will probably be the next most important position, one where both the helmsman and navigator are able to share the view. Most radars have the control panel integral with the display. This poses a dilemma because you want to mount the radar where both helmsman and navigator can view it and allow space for the chart table in front of it, whilst still being able to reach the control panel for adjustments. There is a strong case for having one of the few radars on the market where controls and display can be separated and then you have full freedom to mount each in the optimum position.

Modern radars which use a raster scan display allow daylight viewing under most conditions and there is unlikely to be a problem in a closed wheelhouse.

This allows the radar display to be placed in the best position for both helmsman and navigator to view it simultaneously, a distance from it of around three feet being about right. With an open steering position you have the problem of protecting the screen from bright sunlight and water, so in an existing boat the best solution is to fit the radar under the windscreen with a viewing hood attached. If you have freedom to plan the layout from scratch, then an electronics area protected by a top cover with the instruments let into the fascia can be a good solution to the problems of both sunlight and water.

When an electronic chart system is installed then this should be alongside the radar. Ideally the two displays should be on the same scale and the same heading and then it is possible to make a direct comparison between them and have all the information you need for safe navigation at high speed. The controls of the electronic chart plotter will not need to be accessed so frequently as those of the radar, which is why the electronic chart should be on

The cockpit of a fast racing boat where space can be limited. Note the two compasses in front of the driver, one a standard magnetic compass and the other electronic with left/right indicator. The charts are taped down and there is also a list of the course marks, courses and distances.

the side away from the helmsman, although ideally a system with separate controls and display is still highly desirable.

The final piece of electronic equipment to consider is the position-fixing system. If you have this without the electronic chart plotter then it will take its place alongside the radar to give its bearing, distance and cross track information. When a full range of electronic equipment is fitted, the information shown on the position-fixing equipment is often repeated on the electronic chart and possibly on the radar as well. This means that the position-fixing equipment can be placed where it is convenient to operate the controls rather than to view the display. It is now possible to get repeaters so that vital information can be presented at the helm position as well as in the navigation area.

The more equipment you have the greater will be the competition for space around the navigation area. In addition to the equipment you have to bear in mind the requirements of radars and autopilot. Try to decide at the outset what you plan to install even if you don't fit it all at one go. Then you can look very carefully at how and where you will install each item, trying out all the options before settling for what seems the best solution.

With an existing boat you will be limited by the space available and what is already fitted, but with a new boat a mock-up can be built to get things right. This is well worth while because it is only by meticulous attention to detail that you will achieve a layout which will allow you to use the equipment to its best advantage and have all the information you need when travelling at high speed.

VISIBILITY

Despite this emphasis on the instruments, visibility from the wheelhouse should not be ignored. You will still need eyeball navigation to confirm what the instruments are telling you, and of course you need to keep an eye open for other craft which can approach very rapidly. There are two aspects to visibility, one being the actual area of the horizon that you can see and the other being the quality of the vision.

In a fast boat you almost invariably need something between your eyes and the blast of wind outside. At speeds over 30 knots it only takes a few seconds for your eyes to start watering in the wind, and then your visibility is cut right down to the point where you are almost blind. There are two ways to maintain visibility in this situation, one being to wear glasses or goggles and the other being to look through a window or windscreen.

In some respects you are better off behind a windscreen because in the open, even when you are wearing glasses or goggles, your head is being buffeted by the wind and the resulting quick movements can reduce your ability to see clearly. The bouncing of the boat can have the same effect to a certain extent. However, protection close to your eyes will generally give you better visibility than looking through a windscreen so there are compromises to be made here.

There are two main problems with windscreens, one being reflections on the screen and the other being rain or spray. The reflections come from the angled screen acting like a partial mirror and showing tenuous images of the dashboard underneath. The reflections are at their worst on a sunny day when the flat surfaces under the screen are white and when the screen is tinted glass. Under these conditions clear vision ahead can be severely restricted. This problem can be alleviated by painting all flat reflective surfaces matt black, but this may not be acceptable from an aesthetic point of view. Another solution is to have a windscreen which is vertical or even raked forward at the top but again aesthetics may not allow this. Painting the dashboard black can also help but will not prevent the reflection of lights at night.

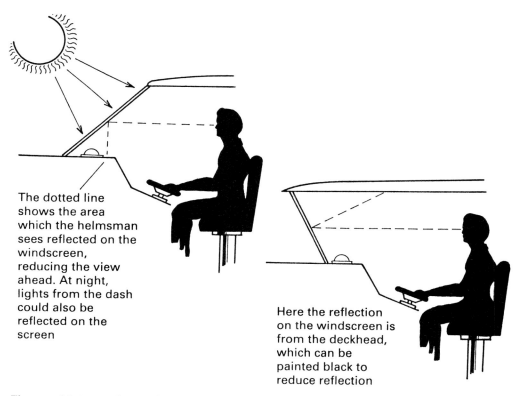

The dotted line shows the area which the helmsman sees reflected on the windscreen, reducing the view ahead. At night, lights from the dash could also be reflected on the screen

Here the reflection on the windscreen is from the deckhead, which can be painted black to reduce reflection

The sun shining on the windscreen can cause reflections from the dash. A forward sloping screen can be one answer.

Water on the screen can be handled by wipers, but it is not always easy to find wipers which remain effective when there is plenty of water hitting the screen. The worst situation is light spray on a sunny day – the spray dries and the wipers smear the remaining damp salt on the screen. Windscreen washers using fresh water can help but you will need plenty of fresh water to keep the screen clear and this may not be acceptable on a fast boat where weight can be a critical factor. One of the best solutions I have found is to spray or cover the screen with a film of one of the proprietary silicone compounds. These stop the water from sticking to the screen so that it gets blown off leaving virtually no salt residue, and the wipers can still be used when there is heavy water. The silicone film seems to last a long time – at least one season.

These methods are necessary with a closed wheelhouse, but with an open steering position you have more choice. Careful siting of the top edge of the screen can allow you to look over the screen when standing and look through the screen when sitting. If the design of the windscreen and its location in the boat are carefully developed you will find that the air flow over the screen leaves a space where your head is protected but where you can still see over the screen. This type of development is rarely carried out by designers or builders of fast boats, but the results are well worth the trouble.

Operating in a closed wheelhouse, visibility to the sides and aft is important both for navigation and collision avoidance. There may be craft out on the water even faster than you and thus overtaking. When you are leaving the land it can be helpful to see where you have come from if only to check on the range of visibility. You don't need an extensive view aft, but you do need a certain amount. An alternative can be to fit wing mirrors as in a car, but these need to be reasonably large, perhaps truck mirror size, and they can be difficult to keep clear.

Both to the sides and to the front the windows have to be divided up to reduce panel size to maintain strength adequate to resist the impact of solid water. Builders and designers tend to take the easy option by allowing wide pillars between the window panels and these can seriously restrict vision. The situation is not helped on some pleasure craft when curtains are fitted to give privacy in harbour, but if you are to read the waves and navigate safely you need all the visibility you can get and few compromises should be made in this area.

Misting up of the wheelhouse windows can affect the visibility very seriously. It is mainly a problem in the winter when all the windows and doors may be shut. Ventilation is the only solution and if you can't open doors or windows then a blower directing preferably warm air on to the windows is the answer.

INTEGRATING WHEELHOUSE REQUIREMENTS

Putting together a workable wheelhouse layout will depend a great deal on what the boat is designed to do. With patrol boats, pilot boats and most commercial craft the wheelhouse tends to be the centre of activity and more effort can be concentrated on its function. Yet it is in these types of craft that tradition and convention seem to have a tight hold and there is less initiative for change. On pleasure craft where there is a much more open approach to design and layout aesthetics tend to be much more important than practicability. The emphasis seems to be on surrounding the crew with instruments and dials to impress rather than help.

It is only in racing boats that there is a much more functional approach to the layout. Here the crew are working at the extremes of speed and difficult conditions, and the resulting layouts show just what can be achieved. There may not be quite the same motivation for this approach at lower speeds, but the benefits in terms of operational capability or pleasure can be almost as great.

A tidy fast boat installation, the main criticism being that the controls for radar and plotter cannot be easily reached, nor is the vertical steering wheel the best type for steering a fast boat.

One approach to try to accommodate some of the compromises which have to be made is to have two control positions so that the open position with its good visibility is used for manoeuvring in harbour and the closed position is used at sea, with the instrumentation allocated accordingly. Such an arrangement can give more options, but the instrumentation and layout need to be designed with just as much care. One interesting aspect when looking at these alternatives is that you are very unlikely to drive a boat so hard from an open position as you are from a closed one. Somehow, the reduced noise and separation from the wind and sea allow you to have less regard for their effects. Perhaps it is just that the additional sensory perception of the sea builds up a greater level of caution. The same effect is noticeable in cars.

The aim in developing the layout is to have all the controls — and that includes the instrument controls — within reach, whilst having the required displays easily visible without conflicting with the need to have a good view of the outside world. The cockpit style layout is the one to aim for and this can combine the aesthetic requirements with the practical. It is worth looking at how things are arranged in cars and aircraft to develop ideas. The large size of much of the electronic instrumentation and the lack of standardised shapes can make it difficult to get a fully integrated look, but in most cases considerable improvements can be made on current arrangements.

Steady improvements are being made in the design of electronic equipment and we will look at these in the next chapter, but the concept of such equipment is also changing. Instead of a multitude of displays such as compass, log, echo sounder, radar, chart, etc., the first steps are being taken towards displaying all of the required information on a couple of VDU screens. With a separate control panel being used to call up the required information for display, the stage is then set for achieving the type of integrated layout which is lacking in many current designs. The main problem, realised by many equipment manufacturers, is just where the initiative for this development is going to come from. In the meantime it is worth looking at the design of such equipment in more detail in order to identify what is good and bad in terms of current design.

8 Instrument design and installation

When you see a piece of navigation equipment standing on its own in the showroom, everything seems so plausible. Follow detailed instructions about installation and very soon you can have the equipment working on your boat. As far as the manufacturers are concerned that tends to be the end of the story, but in reality that is the point at which the inadequacies of the equipment start to show up and where you will begin to notice many little points about the design which could be improved. In the fast boat environment these little inadequacies can assume much larger proportions because everything becomes much more critical.

The problems with much marine electronic equipment seem to stem from the design process. A great deal of thought goes into the development of the software, the operating system of most marine electronics. But when it comes to packaging the electronic circuitry off-the-shelf control panels and displays are used because manufacturers claim that the market is too small to justify custom-made pieces – a retrograde but not irredeemable step. The main problems seem to lie in the box which has to house the unit. This generally *is* custom-made judging by the logos with which they are embellished and the design is finalised before the unit is evaluated at sea. Now it is too late for change, so the evaluation tends to be really a matter of whether the equipment works and whether it stands up to the marine environment.

We will look at some of the areas where there is room for improvement. This will help you select the best equipment for fast boat use even if it is not the best that could be produced.

RELIABILITY

In my experience, most electronic equipment is very reliable as far as the circuitry is concerned. Occasionally there can be problems in the software, although the manufacturers go to great lengths to iron these out. However, commercial pressures can dictate that the software is not entirely free from bugs before marketing, and it is not unusual to find updates in the software being introduced quietly for a couple of years or so after the equipment is launched to help iron out some of the software problems. This means that it can be a good idea not to buy new equipment straight after it hits the market but to wait a year or two.

Much of the trouble with the earlier generations of electronics was due to mechanical failure. Before the introduction of software-based electronics there was a higher proportion of mechanical parts which contributed to the failure rate. Today the main mechanical parts are the nuts, bolts and screws which hold the components together. Under the high vibration levels found on fast boats these components can shake loose and cause trouble. Apart from ensuring that all of these bits are screwed up tight, the only other solution is to put a drop of superglue on the thread, but then the service agent won't thank you when he has to take things apart. What you really need to do before you buy is to take the unit apart and check how the nuts, bolts and screws are secured.

This look at the mechanical components should include a look at the case and its fastenings. I have had a plastic case break away from its mountings simply because it was only secured by plastic studs. Under the impact loadings on a fast boat these could not stand the strain and the unit came adrift. Some of the trunion mounting systems are not very robust either, and even when they stay in place it can be irritating to have the mounting nuts coming loose when they don't lock adequately.

Another thing to look for if you open up the case is how the printed circuit (PC) boards are fixed. In many cases they will just be secured at each end with a considerable unsupported area in the middle. Ideally this type of board should be mounted vertically where it can stand the fast boat pounding without bending. A PC board which is continually flexing will almost certainly give trouble sooner or later. Best of all get a unit where the PC boards are well supported. This will denote quality and show that corners have not been cut. It is surprising how manufacturers cut corners in this way with the hardware when the major cost of the unit is in developing the software. Another cost short cut to look for is plugs which are not locked in place when secured. These will surely come adrift at some point in time if they are of the push fit type.

POWER SUPPLIES

One of the main causes of faults in electronic equipment is not in the equipment itself but in its power supply. Here again manufacturers seem to have a rather casual approach, but this is often matched by the installer. I think this attitude stems from the preaching of generations of instructors who have put forward the gospel that electronics are unreliable, so your navigation should not rely on them. I disagree. Electronics can be reliable if you take trouble in selecting and installing them, and you can certainly rely on them in the same way as you rely on a compass, having options at the back of your mind if things do go wrong. It is only by adopting this attitude that you will get full benefit from your electronics.

The first requirement for the power supply is to get reliable wiring circuits to feed the electronics. The wiring should be installed to the highest marine standards with a switch and fuse incorporated for each piece of equipment. If you can, separate the power supply to the navigation electronics from those which supply the engine ignition and radios. In both of these cases you can get power surges when the starters or radio transmitters are used. An even better system is to have a battery reserved just for the electronics, but even with such a system you can still get surges from the charging circuits which can upset the delicate electronic circuits; you might like to install one of the proprietary systems designed to smooth out the electrical supply.

Even with these standards of installation there will always remain the worry of a power failure, and it is surprising that manufacturers do not address this problem in more detail. Portable computers are available with rechargeable batteries which are charged every time the unit is plugged into the power supply. If this comparatively low cost feature was added to position-fixing receivers, not only would it allow power to be maintained in the event of an electrical failure, but it would also help to isolate these sensitive receivers from the surges and spikes in voltage which can occur in boat power supplies. There are units on the market which do incorporate such batteries, but the aim here is to provide portability rather than reliability. The market at present is bemused by the novelty of electronics, but I suspect that the next generation of marine electronic equipment will be aimed at a market which is much more informed and selective.

Another option open to you to improve the continuity of the power supplies is to have two alternative supplies to the vital electronics via two different circuits from two different banks of batteries. A double pole switch can be incorporated to enable the power to be drawn from one circuit or the other. Whilst there would obviously be a temporary interruption in the supply this shouldn't be enough for the position finding receivers to lose track and prevent them from re-acquiring the signal and position automatically once the power is restored.

FUSES

Fuses are a vital part of the power supply system, but also the cause of many of the problems. In my experience, 50 per cent or more of the problems with electronic equipment can be traced to the fuses, which is both reassuring and worrying. The reassuring part comes from the fact that in all probability, by the fuse blowing, other sensitive parts of the circuitry have been protected. The worrying part is that changing a fuse on many pieces of modern electronics is a far from easy task.

Two fuses are usually involved in protecting the electronics. One is in the main power supply system and may protect two or three units at the one time. It is best for each piece of electronic equipment to have its own circuit and fuse and then the fuse rating can closely match the equipment it has to protect. Such fuses will always have a higher rating than the fuse which is incorporated into the equipment itself, and the manufacturers will have matched this fuse closely to the circuits it has to protect. It is probable that it will be this internal fuse which will blow in the event of a short circuit or other overload, and many manufacturers specify quick-blow fuses which disconnect the circuit in microseconds to prevent damage.

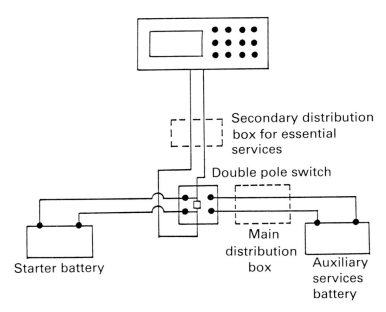

How to rig an alternative power supply from the starter battery for electronic position-finding equipment. The double pole switch allows the alternative battery to supply the essential services.

A fuse, particularly the quick-blow type, is a sensitive device and is thus prone to mechanical failure. The current-sensitive wire in the fuse is held by a spring so that the ends separate rapidly with an overload, but all fuses can be subject to premature failure in the fast boat environment with the pounding generated stresses to which the fuse won't necessarily respond too well. An alternative to the fuse is the circuit breaker, the advantage of which is that when it breaks the circuit, restoring the current is simply a matter of connecting the switch again. Early circuit breakers were too sensitive to the pounding of the boat, but modern units are reliable and are a good investment for fast boats. However, it is not these fuses and breakers which are the main problem areas, but those incorporated into the electronic units themselves.

Here fuses are almost invariably used, probably because they are cheaper. This may be fair enough, but the problem is that the fuse is installed either at the back of the unit, or worse still, inside. I have spend half an hour taking a satnav receiver to pieces to get access to the fuse which had blown, and on a boat rolling at sea this is no easy task. It would be virtually impossible when the boat is travelling at speed, so make sure when you buy equipment that the fuse is on the outside. Even then the problem is not solved because it is often not easy to get access to the back of the unit, and if it is panel-mounted then you have a dismantling job on your hands. It seems that in the quest for cheapness, manufacturers are taking the easy option by installing the fuse where it is convenient for them rather than convenient for replacement at sea. I don't know of any marine equipment where the fuse is in the front panel where it ought to be, but hopefully in time a more practical approach to the design of marine electronics will be adopted. At present, all you can do is grin and bear it, and try and minimise the problem when installing the equipment.

DISPLAYS

There is a choice of displays available on modern marine electronics, with cost being the main factor affecting that choice as far as the manufacturers are concerned. From the user's point of view the main criterion is the visibility of the display under the difficult viewing conditions, with the size of the digital letters and figures being critical. In the quest to include as much information on the display as possible, the trend is towards smaller scale digital information which can merge into a blur at high speed. There is no doubt in my mind that the best display for high speed use is the one with the largest letters and figures, even if this does limit the information available on a single screen. Some of the more sophisticated equipment allows you to select the character size in recognition of the requirements of fast boats, but generally you are stuck with what you have.

The main types of display are the light emitting diode (LED), the liquid crystal display (LCD), and the video screen. The LED is falling out of favour mainly because it has a limited display capability, but the display is bright, can be seen in daylight but can also be dimmed for night use. The LCD is more flexible, is cheap, and is probably the most widely used type of display. It comes in a range of qualities, with the higher cost units giving a greater contrast and a wider angle of view. Apart from its comparatively low cost and its compact size, the LCD also has the merit of being very flexible in the way it can be used. Such displays form the basis of some elementary plotters and even one low cost radar, but their primary use is for the display of digital information. They do not have the sensitivity for displaying detailed graphical information, although the resolution is improving and we may see larger LCD screens in the future.

The display which forms the basis of most radars, plotters and electronic charts is the video display or CRT. Here the required images are formed on the screen of a cathode ray tube in the same way as the image is projected on to a

An alternative place for some instrumentation is above the windscreen. This helps to relieve the dashboard clutter.

TV or computer screen. This gives almost total flexibility in what can be projected onto the screen, with colour, digital information and graphics all being available. The only limitation is the pixel count of the screen, these being the number of horizontal lines to give the vertical definition and the number of dots per line to give the horizontal definition. For marine radar and plotter use, these figures tend to be higher than those on TV screens to give good resolution, but such quality costs money, particularly when larger sizes of screen and colour are involved.

Another problem with video displays is their physical size. This relates not just to the screen size but also to the rear of the tube, which means that equipment incorporating these tubes is never compact in terms of depth. This is not a major problem if the equipment is designed into the wheelhouse, but it makes installation at a later date difficult. Alternative 'flat screen' displays are under development and trial, and it seems likely that such screens will be used in the future, so that the electronic chart will take up little more space than its equivalent paper chart. The flexibility of this type of display will make it the front runner in terms of marine displays and we are already seeing both radar and electronic chart displays in this format being used to display digital information culled from other sources.

In terms of fast boat use, the video display has many advantages, but it is rarely used to its full capabilities. Certainly the display of information in graphical form tends to be easier to understand at a quick glance, but this probably reflects the bad design, layout and presentation of digital information. The designers' aim seems to be to impress rather than inspire, so that as much digital information as possible is squeezed on to the otherwise unused corners of the screen. Small figures which are difficult to read in a fast boat are used to enable more information to be presented, and whilst the aim is to try and give the navigator all the information he needs on one screen, the result tends to confuse rather than help.

The main problem is not so much the displays themselves but rather the way they are used. There is little attempt at integration of the information, and where this is attempted then it generally only serves to repeat information already displayed on other equipment. What is needed are displays which give the navigator precise and clear information in the form he needs it, but so long as a range of different equipment is made in different forms by different manufacturers, then we are still some way from achieving that ideal.

In terms of the ideal arrangement for a fast boat, I visualise three video displays. Two of these would be the electronic chart and the radar, preferably mounted side by side and with the same heading reference. Digital information such as cross track error, scales in use, and course and distance to the

next waypoint could be included on these displays, but this digital information should be kept simple and in large figures which can easily be read. There
would be alternative 'pages' available on the electronic chart screen for more
detailed navigation information and for route planning and waypoint plotting.
Above these two displays could be the third smaller video display which would
show the compass heading in digital and graphical form, and log, sounding
and engine rpm information. This would need careful design to avoid
confusion; colour could be one way of differentiating between the different
types of information.

To this type of three-screen display could be added a fourth for fuel and
engine monitoring, but the basic concept of taking information from a variety
of sources and displaying it in the optimum manner is what counts. This type
of approach is already being adopted for big ship electronics, but the
cost-conscious and fragmented approach to small boat electronics is tending
to retard this type of development. Behind this form of display is a computer
which controls the integration, and fears have been raised that loss of this
computer would mean loss of the whole system. This need not be the case if the

The dashboard on a fast boat with radar and plotter on the left and Loran
C to the right. Compass and log are on the centre line.

system is carefully designed and redundancy is built in.

On a more practical note, most of the displays currently in use are generally reliable even in the fast boat environment. I have not experienced failure with any type of display, except with video displays which were not marinised. Ordinary computer-type video screens are probably more vulnerable but I would expect this to be a mechanical rather than an electronic problem. There is a temptation to use personal computers on board, but one of the major problems is securing them adequately and marinising such units usually involves repackaging the electronics and the display to suit the environment.

REFLECTIONS

The flat screen of the displays of electronic equipment can be a source of irritating reflections, particularly in bright sunlight. In an open steering position the sun may reflect off the screen, but the main problem is that the screen reflects the face of the person looking into it, or the surroundings. If these are brightly lit, then it can be very difficult to see the display itself even when it is turned up to full brilliance. Even a hood over the screen does not really solve the problem, but you may be able to improve things by looking from a different angle or changing the angle of the screen if it is trunion mounted. The best solution from the design point of view is to fit a screen of non-reflective glass. This is more expensive and doesn't entirely solve the problem but it certainly helps. From the point of view of installation you can paint the areas behind the user a dull black if that is practical, and be conscious of the problem of reflections when locating the equipment. The angle of the screen will dictate what it reflects, the best angle probably being as near vertical as is practical.

CONTROLS

Just as the display must be arranged and organised so that you can view it properly, so the controls should be constructed and located so that you can use them easily. Few of the control panels are geared to the requirements of fast boats. Many of the problems stem from the fact that you cannot easily reach out to the controls and that you do not always have the full control over the movement of your hands and fingers that you would like. This can make it difficult to find the correct button when you want to adjust or change the display, and to keep your finger on the button whilst the adjustment is made.

Push buttons are now widely used and most of these are of the membrane type. Control panels of this sort are simple from the manufacturers' point of view, it being possible to mark the membrane cover for the particular application whilst retaining the standard push button panel underneath. They have the benefit of being made easily splashproof, but as there is no positive position for the push button it is not easy to locate your finger on the correct spot and keep it there. Using such panels in a fast boat can be a frustrating experience.

Membrane panels can be improved by having a raised grid over the membrane as part of the case moulding. This gives each button a more positive location and allows you to position your finger. The alternative is the raised button which is easier to locate, but needs to be of adequate size and well spaced so that you can locate the one you want positively and easily. A recess on the top of the button also helps to keep your finger in position.

It helps to have some indication when the push button has actually made contact, particularly if you need to give two or more pushes in succession. A small audible beep is one way, but the noise is often lost in the ambient noise of the boat underway. The alternative is some form of tactile indication such as a positive click when contact is made. You don't want the push buttons to be too sensitive anyway otherwise the merest touch will change the display and it will be too easy to make mistakes. Rotating knobs are easy to use on fast boats provided that they are of adequate size and do not rotate too freely. The control needs a little frictional resistance so that you don't rotate it involuntarily. A large size also gives you more sensitive control.

One of the main problems with control panels on most marine electronics is the size of the equipment. As the electronics become more and more compact, the tendency is to make the control panel smaller which does not help when using the equipment on fast boats. If anything they need to be larger to be easier to use, but that is expensive and so is unlikely to happen. Another problem for left-handed people is that the control panel is usually mounted to the right of the display which means that such people have to put their arms across the display to reach the panel.

On some of the larger equipment such as radars and plotters the control panel can be separated from the display so that it can be mounted for easy use. Even then you ideally want somewhere to rest the ball of your hand to steady it whilst you reach for the control buttons with your fingers. Another alternative – also good for position-fixing receivers and similar instruments – is to fix a handhold from which you can extend your fingers to the control panel. I have used such a system at 90 mph in a racing boat with great success. Generally you can't do much about modifying the equipment once you have bought it, but you can do quite a lot to make it easier to use by careful installation and fixing handholds, etc.

LIGHTING

The lighting of instruments for night use is a difficult matter. You want the screen as bright as possible for easy viewing, but you don't want it to contrast too much with the dark outside to ruin your night vision. Illumination of the controls is just as important so that you can find them in the dark, and this is an area which generally does not receive the attention it deserves, partly because fast boats tend to operate much less at night and partly because to do a good job on night lighting costs money.

Ideally the illumination of all displays, controls, compasses, etc., should be variable in intensity so that the right setting can be selected for the ambient conditions. The dimming on each piece of equipment should be controllable independently so that you can adjust each level to suit. On electronic instruments you have to put up with what the manufacturer gives you, but when it comes to switches, compasses and dials you have more control. Here there are two options; one is to have variable illumination from above (and this can be good for switches such as those for the wipers) and the other is internal illumination which is certainly best for the compass. You may be able to group many of these together linked to the same variable control, but the compass should have its own illumination control.

Manufacturers vary in their approach to the illumination of electronics. Some provide no lighting at all for the control panel; on others there is no adjustment for the display illumination. One reason for these economies is that instruments tend to be made for both power and sailing craft. On the latter, the power consumption can be vitally important and the lighting tends to be a major power consumer. There are few inhibitions about power consumption on a powerboat, so go for the instruments specially made for this purpose if you can. Another reason for the economies in the lighting is cost. In general, if you want adequate lighting you need to go for more expensive equipment, although this is not always the case. Some manufacturers argue that to light control panels adequately can introduce R/F interference into the sensitive electronics which is why they don't do it. In this case the answer is to rig external lighting because if you need to see the panel markings in the daytime you also need to see them at night.

Control lighting is easier to engineer with a membrane panel than with individual buttons or knobs. It is not just the button which needs illumination but also its function. The design of the equipment and its lighting clearly needs very careful consideration for fast boat navigation.

INTERFERENCE

When you have an array of electronic instruments in the wheelhouse you have to address the problems of interference. We have already looked at the magnetic interference between electronics and the magnetic compass in Chapter 6, but interference also occurs between the electronic units themselves. The equipment most at risk here is the Loran C and Decca Navigator receivers, but anything which has a computer inside is at risk, and that applies to most electronics. Interference can come from a variety of sources. Radios, particularly powerful MF or HF radios can create strong interference when transmitting. The ignition systems on petrol engines are another offender, but even CRT displays can generate interference. Distance is the easy solution if you have space to separate units, but the principal solution is to screen and earth all the sensitive cables and equipment.

Fortunately with modern radios the transmitter can now be installed separately from the control panel, so it can be placed away from the wheelhouse to reduce interference. Ignition systems should have full suppression systems fitted, and all of the electronic instruments should be fully earthed to help isolate them from interference. Good electronic equipment tends to have a metal case which can also help to reduce interference if it is properly earthed. When you open up equipment you will often find metal screening boxes inside. Fully screened coaxial cable should be used for the links which connect the various pieces of electronics and for all antenna cables. In the wheelhouse itself try to separate CRT displays from the Loran and Decca receivers, particularly if you use a PC type computer which is not suppressed to marine standards.

ANTENNAE

With the expanding use of electronics, finding space for all the antennae can be a problem. Again for Loran and Decca, it is the antennae which are the sensitive parts as far as interference is concerned so they should be mounted as far as possible from any transmitting antennae such as radar and radios. The best solution is to separate the antennae into passive and active so that they can be mounted in two groups. Amongst the passive antennae will be the Loran, Decca, satnav, weather fax and navtex. These are receive-only antennae which will generate little or no interference. The satnav antenna should have a clear, all round 'view' of the horizon because it needs a direct link to the satellite. Active antennae, particularly those for the MF or HF radio, should be removed as far as possible from the passive antennae, although radar and VHF antennae are not so critical.

Keep the passive antennae as far away from the engines as possible, particularly when you have petrol engines. Outboards in particular seem to generate a high level of interference, but it is possible to buy special paints which can be applied to the inside of the outboard hood to cut down the interference. Before finalising the position of Loran or Decca antennae, mount them temporarily in different positions and check the signal-to-noise ratio on the instrument. Do this with the engines running at cruising speed, and also see what the effect is when radio and radar are used. In this way you can find the best position for the antennae where the interference is at an acceptable level.

Whip antennae are commonly used for boat installations, but these are not always suitable for high performance craft. Shorter stub antennae are available which can stand high speed stress better, and for Loran and Decca an alternative is to use antennae designed for aircraft use.

MOUNTING

Most boat electronics come with a trunion mounting enabling the equipment to be installed at different angles. An alternative is to panel mount the equipment which makes for a tidier installation but can make the fuses and connections difficult to get at if there are problems at sea.

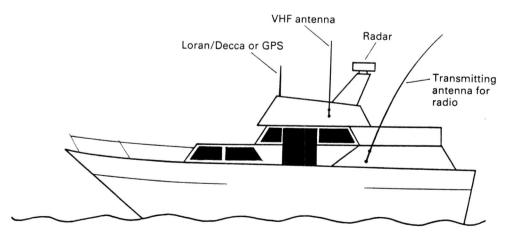

Locating the antennae for electronic instrumentation in the correct place can avoid interference between the equipment. As a general rule transmitting antennae linked to radios should be remote from passive antennae such as position-fixing equipment.

It would seem logical to use flexible mounts on sensitive electronic equipment to reduce the effects of impact and vibration. In my experience, flexible mounting is not very satisfactory, largely I think because such mountings can only be designed to damp out one particular frequency whilst on a fast boat there can be a whole variety. With flexible mounting the equipment seems to move around more than would seem wise for it, but perhaps more importantly, this movement can make it difficult to read the display.

Rigid mounting seems to work despite the shock loadings imposed. Even when equipment is subject to stresses under which the human body starts to complain, good quality equipment seems to survive, so rigid mounting is recommended although a firm rubber insert between the equipment and its mounting panel can help absorb the worst of the shocks. If the equipment doesn't cope then it could be argued that it is not suitable for fast boat use.

There is still a long way to go in the design and installation of equipment to enable it to survive in the fast boat environment. Much of the development

Twin radars and position fixing receivers give a measure of redundancy, so that you still receive information even when things go wrong.

works lies in the hands of the manufacturers, but there is still a lot that you as the user can do to improve the situation. Only when the equipment can be used properly will you be able to get the best out of it. Electronics have a major contribution to make to fast boat navigation so it is worth taking trouble.

9   The human element

At some time in the future we might well find a strong measure of automation coming into fast boat navigation. Until that time arrives the human element will have a very important role to play, acting as the interface between the information provided by the navigation systems and the controls of the boat. In all present day navigation of fast boats this interface is vital and largely determines not only the speed of the boat if conditions are at all difficult, but also the safety.

Such is the progress with fast boat design today that the weak link in the system tends to be the human component. From a safety point of view this is excellent, because if the human gives up first, or at least feels the need to ease back, then the boat will be inherently safe. However, this safety aspect may apply to the boat's structure and equipment – the human feeling the stress before the structure – but it doesn't necessarily apply to the navigation. Indeed it could be argued that because the human is feeling under stress and needs to reduce speed, then the ability to carry out the required navigation tasks is reduced and mistakes could be made, putting the boat at risk.

This is a situation which calls for compromise. You could try to make life so comfortable for those on board that they can navigate with confidence whilst at the same time being isolated from the effects of the outside world. To a certain extent you see this in modern offshore racing boats with totally enclosed cockpits where the crew are comfortably seated and firmly strapped in place. Here you feel much more confident about navigating and it is much easier to concentrate on the job in hand without having to spend a large proportion of your time hanging on tightly. Travelling at speeds of around 120 mph you need to have this confidence in navigation, particularly when you are relying on eyeball navigation. At two miles a minute things happen very quickly on the navigation front. However, the problem is that when you are cocooned in a capsule in this way you can also become over-confident in your ability to drive the boat. The capsule is designed to offer you a degree of safety if things go wrong, but isolated from the wind and sea noise, you are tempted to push the boat much closer to the limits than with a more conventional open cockpit. The sprung seating and tight harness also tends to distance you from the movement of the boat, all of which can be a bonus in the competitive world of offshore racing where you need to drive as close to the limits as possible in order to be successful. In the more routine world of fast boat navigation, improving the navigation environment can be a great help in enabling you to cope with difficult conditions, but it is also important to understand the weaknesses of the human element and how this might affect your ability to navigate and control the boat.

MENTAL ATTITUDE

Your mental attitude to the problem is vitally important and here motivation can play a strong part. It is not too difficult to cope with the two or three hours of high speed discomfort in an offshore racing boat when you know that success awaits you at the end. Such an experience has reasonably finite limits and the timescale is about the maximum you can cope with. A fast boat proceeding at more moderate speeds over the same distance could double the journey time whilst still producing similar levels of discomfort, and here mental stress can play a much more significant role. You will have the option of slowing or stopping to ease the strain in the short term, but in the long term this only prolongs the agony unless you cut the trip short. Again it is a question of motivation, and it is surprising what you can cope with if you have a good enough reason for doing so.

Physical and mental stress go closely hand in hand in a fast boat which is one of the reasons why I place so much emphasis on getting the wheelhouse layout just right and having instruments which you can operate comfortably. This helps to reduce the physical stress, particularly if you have good seating, and this will improve your ability to cope with the navigation. One of the vital aspects of fast boat navigation is concentration, and you will only be able to concentrate on the job in hand if you keep the physical stress under control.

In a racing boat with an open cockpit travelling at high speed I would estimate that you are only working at around 50 per cent of your normal mental ability. The rest is given over to coping with the physical stresses of the situation. It is easy to see how you can make mistakes in this situation, and it is only by trying to shut off the physical aspects and trying to cope with the job in hand, that you can hope to concentrate adequately. At lower speeds the ratio changes for the better, but it can still be demanding, with the ratio changing for the worse with the passage of time. Apart from the basic layout and design of the working environment, the other aspect which enables you to cope is having prepared the navigation in advance as far as possible. Knowing where you are going can do a lot to reduce the mental stress, and this is also why electronics can be such a tremendous help in fast boats.

ROUGH SEAS

In a fast boat, rough seas can increase the mental and physical strain dramatically. You tend to think only about the next wave ahead as the boat bangs and crashes its way through the water. To think further ahead means having to consider the implications of further pain and discomfort, yet as a navigator your job entails thinking ahead to the destination and how to get there. At least you are aware of how long it will take to get to calmer waters, but this has both its good and bad sides.

In rough sea conditions you can quickly become tired or even exhausted from the constant strain of having to hang on against the movement of the boat. In this condition you can be tempted to take risks in order to reduce your

The skipper of a fast boat needs a carefully designed environment if he is to be fully in control of the situation. Here most of the vital items are within easy reach.

exposure to the situation, taking short-term risks for a long-term gain. For instance, a situation could arise where there is a harbour close by which could provide relief from the seas outside. However, the entrance could be untenable in the rough conditions perhaps because of a strong ebb tide running against the wind over shallow water. The temptation to overlook these conditions in the entrance will be great with your desire to escape from the conditions outside, and it is easy to convince yourself that you are doing the right thing by attempting the entrance, particularly as you won't see the bad conditions until you are virtually upon them.

Rough seas are physically very tiring in a fast boat with the constant movement contributing to the discomfort. You also need more concentration to drive the boat because you have to watch every wave, assess it and adjust the throttles accordingly. Good wheelhouse design can help to reduce the physical strain, particularly good seating and the use of seat belts, and it is in these conditions that attention to detail in the layout and design of the instrumentation starts to pay off. Even if it doesn't take long for the mental strain to begin to show, the important thing is to be aware of your impaired condition, to concentrate hard and consider the situation very carefully before making important decisions. Once again, preparation will help tremendously in reducing the mental workload. If you have done your homework properly, the decisions should be obvious and there will be less chance of making mistakes.

SEASICKNESS

One of the most serious conditions in which you may have to make rational navigation decisions is seasickness. As a sufferer for 40 years, I am well aware of how seasickness can affect your ability to cope. You will do almost anything to arrive at a situation where the motion of the boat will stop, and of course this can mean taking unnecessry risks. Even your ability to make any decision at all is reduced, and you just want to put your head down and sleep. Recognising the debilitating effect of seasickness both on yourself and the other members of the crew is important. At least then you will be able to make allowances for the situation. Don't ignore a crew member who is seasick, because he could be at risk from injury or even falling overboard; try to make afflicted crew members safe and comfortable so that they won't pose a problem to themselves or the boat.

One of the main causes of seasickness is that the brain is receiving conflicting messages about the movement of the boat. If you are looking inside the boat then your eyes will try to persuade the brain that you are staying level because you are staying level in relation to the boat. However, the balance sensors in your ears will try to convince the brain that the boat is moving about. Confused by the conflicting messages, the brain triggers a signal to the stomach and seasickness is the result. This is not the complete cause of seasickness, but it is the main one and it does offer the possibility of finding solutions.

Obviously, if you can watch the horizon then your brain will receive fewer conflicting messages. This is why people steering a boat are generally less afflicted. The poor old navigator, having to concentrate on the electronic instruments, is in a worse position and could be very susceptible to seasickness, particularly if it means concentrating on the radar in fog, or switching attention from the instruments to the sea outside. Even being in an enclosed wheelhouse can increase the likelihood of seasickness because when you are looking through the windscreen you are still receiving messages of the movement of the boat from your immediate surroundings which can be stronger than those from outside.

Generally, you are much less likely to be seasick in a boat with an open steering position. It is not just the fresh air which makes the difference, but the fact that eyes and ears are giving more cohesive messages to the brain. You may notice that seasickness sufferers tend to want to be outside even though it may be cold and wet, and this is an instinctive reaction to try to improve the situation. Closing your eyes also reduces the confusion and this is why sufferers want to lie down and sleep.

In my experience fast boats are much less likely to cause seasickness, which is probably why I enjoy fast boat navigation. The motion is very different from that of a slow boat – a faster, more jolting movement which perhaps gives the brain less chance to react adversely. It may also be because you have to concentrate harder in a fast boat which gives your brain less time to worry about conflicting messages about the motion of the boat. However, the risk of seasickness increases considerably at night time because you can see little of the outside world and thus the conflicting messages get stronger. You should be aware of this increased risk because darkness brings its own problems with fast boat operations and if you compound these with an increased risk of seasickness then you could be vulnerable at this time.

I find that the proprietary tablets for seasickness work well and it only needs one tablet, taken before you set off, to cope with the problem. After that your body and brain will usually have adjusted to the changing world at sea and the brain will no longer send the trigger messages to the stomach. You are probably most at risk if you leave harbour and go straight into rough seas. Tablets have to be taken about an hour before you are liable to be subject to seasickness so that they can be absorbed; they cannot be taken once you feel sick because your stomach will not accept them. A better solution in my experience is the adhesive patches, like small sticking plasters, which are placed behind the ear. These transdermal patches allow the drug to be absorbed through the skin and can be effective even when you have reached the sickness stage.

One of the main side effects of all seasickness remedies is tiredness. Each comes with a warning that you should not drive machinery after taking the drug – and a boat, particularly a fast boat, is machinery. On balance I think the tiredness is less of a problem than the seasickness, but on a fast boat you must recognise the effects of both these problems, particularly on your ability to make rational decisions. Tiredness can be slept off if you are at sea long enough, whilst with seasickness your ability to cope tends to come in waves. Immediately after the physical act of being sick, you will feel a lot better for a while and this is the time to cope with the navigation, recognising that things will get worse as you approach the next bout of sickness.

Seasickness should not be taken as a sign of weakness; it is quite normal to be seasick, but if you do suffer you should recognise and accept the limitations it can place on your ability to cope with navigation. I would be very concerned with people who try to pretend that everything is normal despite seasickness. It is much better to accept that you will have limitations if you are sick and try and work within them. Once again, preparation can reduce the impact of seasickness on navigation and if you have done your homework properly you will be able to concentrate on the outside world to reduce its impact.

TIREDNESS

Tiredness, like seasickness, is something you can do without when navigating a fast boat. You may be able to reduce the onset of seasickness with medication, but there is no real solution for tiredness except sleep. It is much more insidious because you will not always be aware of its onset and its effect on your decision-making. It is surprising just how long you can keep going without sleep or rest, but your ability to cope will be greatly reduced although you may not recognise it. Even at the end of a two or three hour powerboat race you can find yourself mentally and physically exhausted but this is largely the result of letting go once you have crossed the line and can afford to relax. Up to that point you are probably fully in control.

On a three-day Atlantic record crossing there is no doubting the effects of tiredness, and this is why I had a back-up navigator on shore with whom I could discuss my navigation strategy to avoid making silly mistakes. More conventional fast boats may not have this luxury, and if you plan to be at sea for any length of time then you must pace yourself to ensure that you have reserves for the more difficult navigation sectors. Another reason for having good comfortable seats fitted with harnesses is that you can take short naps, secure in the knowledge that you will not get thrown around the boat if the motion becomes violent. The main problem with tiredness is not so much with the navigation, but with actually driving the boat, for which a higher level of concentration is needed. It is far better to swap drivers at frequent intervals rather than let one person think he can keep going all the time, but here the strategy will depend on the skills and capability of the crew. Above all, don't be tempted to take drugs to relieve tiredness.

FOOD AND DRINK

This subject may seem far removed from fast boat navigation but the availability of food and drink can go a long way to increasing the pleasure of fast boating or enabling you to cope. In tough conditions food and drink can help to convince you that things have not got totally out of hand and can help to restore some feeling of normality. Food will usually be in the form of snacks, sandwiches, etc., whilst drinks will probably have to be cold – hot drinks on a fast boat can be dangerous due to the risk of spillage. Once again preparation is necessary to ensure that the food and drinks are ready before you take off. The best containers for drinks are the cyclists' bottles with a short plastic tube to suck the drink out.

Alcoholic drinks should have no place on a fast boat, at least whilst it is moving. The risks of alcohol on fast boats are just as great as in cars, but it is not just a question of drunken driving. Many people feel that in difficult conditions, cold or rough seas, a quick tot will help them keep going. True, it can give a quick lift, perhaps because it is a sign of some sort of normality if you can have a drink, but the effect is very short lived and in the longer term it will lower your resistance and ability to cope.

The only real way to cope with navigating fast boats from a physical point of view is to be fit. There is no doubt that the fitter you are the better able you will be to handle the tiring effects of the constant motion and still have something in reserve to cope with the mental requirements. Preparation can reduce the mental stress and there is no reason why fast boat navigation should not be an enjoyable and exhilarating experience if you are in the right condition to cope.

10 Navigating at night and in poor visibility

Darkness and fog pose the two main problems for the fast boat navigator just as they do for most marine navigators. However, at night the navigator of a fast boat loses much more of his capability than would be the case on a slower boat. This is largely due to the difficulty of judging distances which is an essential part of the fast boat navigator's repertoire. Combined with this is the fact that most of the navigation lights on buoys and in lighthouses are flashing lights which makes it much harder to keep track of what is going on.

Added to this is the difficulty or impossibility of reading the waves. This is essential for fast boat control and driving a fast boat at night can be likened to driving down an unlit road without headlamps. The only consolation at sea is that there shouldn't be any hard objects to hit if you get things wrong, but hitting a larger than average wave at night is very frightening and if the boat becomes airborne, you wait for what seems like an eternity for the boat to land. In fact it is only a split second, but because you don't know the timing or the outcome of the landing the tensions are very great.

The obvious solution to both of these factors is to slow down, and almost certainly at night you will not travel as fast as you do in the daytime, no matter what the pressure. You can cope with the navigation at night if you concentrate hard and do your preparation, but there is no solution for the rough and unpredictable ride except endurance.

By comparison navigation at speed in fog is comparatively easy, but you do require confidence, concentration and preparation. In the case of the latter you may well want to modify your route in favour of easier landfalls. We will look at the collison avoidance factors in Chapter 11, but for the sake of safety and to conform with the rules of the road it may be necessary to moderate your speed. The range of visibility should be at least twice your stopping distance, and since you can't change the visibility you will have to modify your speed.

The solution to both night and fog navigation in a fast boat is electronics. They overcome so many of the problems that I would consider them essential under these difficult conditions, but first let us look at the technique of navigating without electronics.

EYEBALL NAVIGATION AT NIGHT

Leaving to one side the actual driving of the boat in waves, the main problems you will have to face at night are the absence of many of the features you would use to help fix your position in daylight, the often intermittent positioning of navigation lights, the difficulty in judging distances and the flashing nature of those navigation lights. General lights on the shore can give you an idea of where the land lies and you may even see headlands or other features silhouetted against them but in general shore lights confuse rather than help by making it harder to see some of the navigation lights.

The difficulty in judging distances means that you will have less chance to cut corners and pass close to headlands or other features as you could do in the daytime. The general rule at night is to give everything a wide berth to err on the side of safety, but watch out that this doesn't take you into tide races or other inhospitable waters. Try to plan your route so that you will always have at least one navigation light in sight at all times. You have the consolation that at night the lights will generally show up over greater distances than the features which they would mark in daytime, and this can be helpful with landfalls. Always aim at or near a light, preferably a powerful one, when making a landfall.

In more crowded waters where there may be several lighted buoys marking a channel it can be very confusing at night and this is where you need concentration. You can only identify the buoys by the character and colour of their lights, and it takes time to establish this – time during which you may be rushing towards them at high speed. The apparent brightness of the buoy light does not always mean it is the nearest, so you do need to think on your feet to get the buoys in the right sequence. Try to concentrate on the one you are approaching whilst trying to check out the next one ahead. Do not aim too close to the buoy because you can suddenly find it very close indeed. It can be a good idea to steer the boat on autopilot in this situation. The consistent and steady heading will ensure that the buoy comes up in the same position each time it flashes and you will know where to look for it. Always be ready to slow down if you are not happy with what you see ahead and don't try to make the flashing lights fit what you expect to see. Be sure before you press ahead.

EYEBALL NAVIGATION IN FOG

'Eyeball' is hardly the right term, beccause you will be very restricted in what you can see, but at the end of the day you will still have to rely on seeing some navigation mark or marks to get to your destination. Not only do you need to keep to your track and try to get some clues along the way, but you also have to find the landfall marks at your destination. Without electronics, it will tax your navigation skills to the full.

The important thing once again is preparation: setting a course to take maximum advantage of what is available. The basic requirement is to keep the distance between potentially visible marks as short as possible in order to reduce the risk of errors in the course setting you off track. You should also keep away from inhospitable areas of coastline where there may be rocks and shoals, but clear stretches of coast where you can keep in visual contact with the shore can be very valuable. It is another case of the shortest route not always being the fastest, and deviations can bring greater security to your navigation.

In fog you are relying heavily on steering a straight course for a given time in order to find the next mark. Concentration on the steering is important so that you have some hope of arriving at your destination, and for your time of arrival to be correct you need to run at a consistent speed so that you can work out the

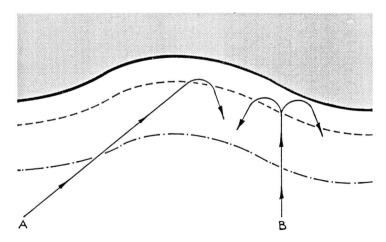

It is much better to approach a coastline at a shallow angle as in A, so that when the soundings decrease you know which way to turn for safety. A direct approach as in B leaves you with two options and a much larger angle to turn through.

distance travelled with some confidence. On this type of 'blind' run you will hopefully hit your next navigation point right on the nose, but try to work out a strategy to cope if it doesn't turn up on time. This might involve making a search either side of the mark when you have run the distance, or aiming for a point of land which is large enough to find even if it takes you a little off course. Do not just steam aimlessly about trying to find the mark because that is the surest way to get totally confused. Remember that most important buoys and lights also have fog signals, so simply stopping the engines and listening may point the way to the mark.

If you are making a landfall in fog then try to aim for a stretch of coastline where there are no offlying shoals or rocks. Here you will be able to approach with a degree of confidence and the echo sounder can give you warning of your approach. It is much better to make a landfall at an oblique angle to the coastline rather than directly at right angles. In the latter case you will not know which is the best way to turn if you see something looming out of the fog and you will have to turn through a full 180 degrees before heading out to sea again. Approaching at an oblique angle you not only slow the approach, but there is only one obvious way to turn out of danger. I once made a 50 mile run along a coastline in fog well offshore because of offlying rocks and shoals and then turned in to make a landfall on a 7 mile long stretch of clear coastline which could be approached with confidence. Even then we ended up at one end of the 7 mile stretch, but we made the landfall which was the important thing.

If you are making a coastal passage aim for a point inside the headland rather than the headland itself so that you can be sure of finding it, but always beware of any offlying dangers. This approach will also keep you out of the main shipping channels which will help with collision avoidance.

In fog your biggest problems will occur when it is also dark. The combination of darkness and fog will stretch you to the limits because you will not be able to see what the visibility limits are, and there is a strong case here for coming right off the plane and playing for safety.

USING ELECTRONICS

When operating at night or in fog your navigation techniques can be under considerable pressure in a fast boat. The best way of reducing the pressures is to use electronics to help navigate with confidence, particularly at night.

Radar is the vital piece of equipment for both these conditions because not only does it show you where you are in relation to the land and navigation marks, but it also shows up other vessels in your vicinity. Radar can indicate where you are going via the heading marker, and although it may not give the total answer it can give you enough assistance to enable navigation to be performed with confidence rather than with hesitation. It supplements the information from other sources to give a much clearer pictures.

At night, radar can restore the vital ability to measure distances. You will know how far you are off a headland and you can plan your route to take advantage of the shortest distances. Using the radar to present a picture of your surroundings and the naked eye to confirm the position of navigation lights will give you most of the information you need for navigation. In buoyed channels, the radar will show where you are in relation to the pattern of buoys so that you can set your course with confidence and identify the buoys as they come up. The location of harbour entrances and piers can be seen often long

Navigating in fog can bring nasty surprises unless you slow down and use radar. Keeping out of the expected shipping lanes will reduce the chance of encounters with ships.

before you can identify them visually. This illustrates one of the big advantages of radar at night: it enables you to work ahead and to have time in hand, taking some of the pressure off you when you are travelling at speed. It can therefore give you the confidence to continue when, without such information, you could be forced to slow down.

In fog the situation is complicated because radar is used for both navigation and collision avoidance. It would be nice to have two radars, one for each role because the two can conflict, but in general collision avoidance should take priority. From the navigation point of view the radar in fog gives you the same confidence level as it does at night because the picture it gives of your surroundings in a world where these are virtually invisible is very helpful. The radar also enables you to establish just exactly what the visibility is so that your speed can be set with greater confidence.

Position-fixing electronics also help a great deal, both at night and in fog. Knowing exactly where you are is vital information when there may not be too many clues from outside. As with general electronic navigation it is the course and distance to the next waypoint and the cross track error which are the important pieces of information, but these are only numbers which you have to translate mentally into a visual picture. The electronic chart can do this for you and the combination of electronic chart and radar should give you all the information you need for navigating in the difficult conditions at night or in fog.

Even with this type of presentation you still need caution. Sea clutter or rain can hide targets on the radar, so that a buoy or even an isolated lighthouse could be hard to find. This is where the electronic chart can help, by showing information which can highlight potential weaknesses in the radar presentation. In this way radar's limitations can be much easier to understand, which is important in fog or at night because this is when everything becomes that bit more critical. Navigating at speed in fog will probably tax your navigation skills to the full and the margins of safety can be smaller. It is up to you to assess just what these margins are and to adjust your speed and navigation accordingly.

It is when you get into these tough conditions that the layout of the wheelhouse and the instrumentation can become critical. At night you have to check on the chart what the characteristics of the navigation lights are and then relate them to what you see outside. (Some electronic chart displays can show these light characteristics.) You need to concentrate on the radar, with a glance every now and then at what the position-fixing equipment is saying. All the time a course has to be steered and, vitally important, a watch has to be kept through the wheelhouse windows.

It is too much for one person to do adequately in fog and, to a certain extent, at night. Navigating a fast boat is a two-person job even when you have an autopilot to help with the steering. One person cannot cope with the radar and other electronics and keep a proper lookout, particularly in crowded waters. In fog there is always the tendency for the lookout to be casual simply because there is nothing to see. The radar picture is always much more interesting and in a darkened wheelhouse the eye tends to be drawn to the radar rather than the blankness of the outside world. It requires a considerable effort of will to keep a lookout at night or in fog, but you ignore this vital aspect of navigation at your peril.

11   *Collision avoidance*

An essential part of navigation is avoiding other craft in your vicinity at sea; the international regulations for prevention of collision at sea cover what action you should take in considerable detail. Whilst these regulations don't make specific allowances for fast craft they are still applicable, and I am certainly not advocating that you depart from these rules in any way. They are law, and you disobey them at your peril. However, there are techniques in which the speed of fast craft can be used to advantage, and in many cases it pays to take the initiative in any collision avoidance situation. The rules allow you to do this provided you do so in good time so as not to cause confusion to the other vessel involved.

You will get no thanks from anyone if you come rushing up to another craft at high speed, apparently on a collision course and then swerve and alter course at the last minute to pass clear. It may give you something of a kick but it will put the other person in quite a panic, particularly if they expect you to be the vessel to give way. You may well find them taking unpredictable action which could lead you both unwittingly into a very close-quarters situation at the last minute. There is nothing wrong with you taking the initiative in a collision avoidance situation, but put yourself in the other person's shoes and make sure that any action you take is very obvious to the other vessel, and as far as possible avoid coming close so that confusion may be avoided.

Despite following the regulations for prevention of collision at sea I have often found that other vessels do not appreciate the speed at which the boat is travelling, particularly a very fast boat. In this situation it is best for you to take avoiding action, which should involve passing around the stern of the other craft where possible rather than passing across its bow. The latter may be the easy option, but if anything should happen to your engines during the critical crossing period you could find yourself in trouble, so passing around the stern is much the safer route to adopt and really takes you very little out of your way. It also appears much better from the point of view of the other vessel and gives its helmsman a greater feeling of security.

Perhaps the biggest risk in any close-quarters situation with other vessels is when you are overtaking, and this can be a frequent occurrence in fast boats. Most vessels tend to keep their lookout concentrating ahead rather than astern, so in a fast boat you can find yourself coming up astern of another vessel without it being aware of your presence until you come rushing by. This is something you should avoid because it could precipitate unpredictable action; the vessel might alter course across your bow without warning, for example. If you find yourself approaching from astern and overtaking another vessel it is your duty to keep clear, but do so in a wide sweep rather than rushing up close alongside.

COLLISION AVOIDANCE AT NIGHT

At night time your approach should be even more cautious. Whilst in the daytime you can easily assess the speed and heading of an approaching vessel, at night you only have the navigation lights to go by and it is nothing like so easy to make an accurate assessment. You obviously have a broad idea about what the vessel is doing by the lights it is showing towards you, but it is here that radar can be a great advantage even when the visibility is clear. Simply by putting the bearing cursor on the approaching vessel you can see if there is risk of collision; once again if you are going to take avoiding action then do so in plenty of time and pass well clear so that the other vessel can appreciate what you are doing.

At night time the other vessel will have even less appreciation of your high speed than in daylight, so you must avoid taking any action which is likely to cause panic. Once again it is when approaching from astern that difficulties can arise, and with your high speed the closing speeds here can be quite high, possibly in the order of 40 knots, which means that you could find yourself very close to the other vessel before you realise it. One of the main difficulties is that you only see a stern light of the vessel ahead and this may not be easily visible or recognisable, particularly in crowded waters, until you are quite close. It is also difficult to judge the distance off and you can suddenly find yourself very close indeed.

Here again radar is the answer. You should be able to relate the light you see ahead to the target you see on the screen and get a much clearer picture of the situation in time to take action to avoid any close-quarters incident.

When talking about collision avoidance we tend to consider only the vessels, but in high speed craft floating debris is also a considerable risk. One of the things you need to do in daytime is keep a watchful eye for any floating debris, and high speed craft are usually manoeuvrable enough to avoid this. Lobster pots and other fishing gear are prime offenders here, and in any encounter with fishing gear high speed boats are likely to come off worse because of the risk of ropes around the propellors.

At night time there certainly won't be lights on any floating debris and it is very unlikely that fishing gear will be lit. Even when fishing gear is lit, it is usually a low powered light which you are only likely to see at the last minute, possibly too late to avoid. There is not much you can do about floating debris because it occurs randomly in the ocean, and this is really a risk that you have to learn to live with if you want to travel at high speed at night. Certainly in my experience it is much less of a risk than might be imagined, and I have never suffered hull damage from collision with floating debris despite many, many thousands of miles of high speed travel both day and night. Fishing gear is a different matter, but it is possible to a certain extent to anticipate where you might find it, either by study of pilotage books or having a basic knowledge of fishing.

There are really two types of fishing gear you need to avoid at night time. The first are lobster and crab pots which tend to be laid in fairly shallow water close to land, and where the seabed is comprised mainly of rocks. There are often patches of lobster pots on rocky outcrops, so the moral here is avoid these areas and generally give this type of coastline a wide berth. The other type of fishing gear, which is much more troublesome, is the drift-nets which are laid out in long lines usually at right angles to the shore for catching fish such as salmon. These drift-nets can be anything up to 5 miles in length and all you see on the surface is a line of floats which support the net.

By the time you have seen these in a high speed boat, it is probably too late to take avoiding action, but with a little luck you can at least stop your propellers to prevent the net getting tangled around them and then hopefully drift across. At night, of course, you won't see them at all, although occasionally these drift-nets are marked with buoys with lights at either end. One would like to hope that similarly lit buoys are located at intervals along the stretch of the net, but in my experience this is not the case. If you expect these fishing nets then the only way to avoid them is to keep further offshore at night time, which seems to be the best bet anyway unless you are familiar with the particular stretch of coast and know where and how these nets might be laid.

COLLISION AVOIDANCE IN FOG

There is one golden rule about navigating at high speed in fog and that is that you should adjust your speed so that the limit of visibility is at least twice your stopping distance. If you take the power off a fast boat it normally stops very rapidly, often within about 100 yards, so this rule is not quite so curbing as might at first be imagined. You need at least twice your stopping distance in terms of visibility because there will obviously be a reaction time before you sight something ahead and before you actually close the throttles or take other avoiding action. Twice the stopping distance should be the absolute minimum – and that is really only applicable to boats equipped with radar. Without radar you will have no clue as to what lies ahead until you see it, so you need that bit more time to assess the situation and take action, so that four or five times the stopping distance would be a good limit for the visibility.

Vessels navigating in fog should make sound signals according to the regulations for prevention of collision at sea. One of the problems on a fast boat is the high noise level which would prevent you hearing any of these sound signals until the other vessel was very, very close. If you want to behave strictly in accordance with the rules then not only must you make sound signals but you must also stop every now and again listen for those of other vessels; if you hear them ahead of your beam then you must navigate with a great deal of caution. In practice, or at least certainly in my experience, very few craft make these sound signals nowadays except perhaps those not equipped with radar who feel a certain nervousness about their exposed position in fog and like to make their presence known. Most boats equipped with radar – and this also applies to many ships – feel that the radar excuses them from making these sound signals and they will only do so when another vessel is close to them which they have already detected on radar.

Radar has really revolutionised the way in which vessels navigate in fog, and in my opinion it would be imprudent for any owner of a fast boat to think they could navigate at speed without it. The way radar is used in poor visibility will depend a great deal on what the visibility is like, the sea conditions, and the manoeuvrability of the craft to which it is fitted. The first and last factors have much in common because if an approaching vessel can be sighted on the radar in good time to take avoiding action then the job of the helmsman is made much easier. All he has to do is note the approaching vessel so that he will pick it up visually at the earliest possible moment and take the necessary avoiding action. It sounds easy, but in fact there can be many drawbacks to this approach which can lead to danger.

The first of these drawbacks is that the range of visibility may fluctuate considerably. One minute you may be able to see for half a mile, which should give you more than ample time to take avoiding action, but what happens if the visibility closes in just when you expect to sight the approaching craft? Then there will be little time to take alternative action and you may make a panic manoeuvre which should be avoided in fog. Very rarely is the visibility constant in fog and you must always be prepared for variations.

Another drawback is that there may be two or more vessels approaching from different directions and your manoeuvre to avoid one might take you into the path of the other. Remember also that you are in a comparatively small craft which may not present a particularly good radar target to the other vessel. They will not thank you for suddenly appearing on their screen a short distance ahead. Remember they don't know what your intentions are or whether you have radar. In bad weather the target presented by your vessel could easily be lost in the sea clutter after they have detected you initially at longer ranges.

Of course the same applies to your radar. There is no guarantee that you will detect all the vessels in your vicinity so you should proceed with a degree of caution and be prepared for the unexpected. The law requires that you keep a good lookout in fog – those that don't deserve the consequences.

We have already looked at using the type of relative motion radar found on most fast boats. With this type of radar there is no quick means of measuring the course and speed of the other vessel, so plotting is the recommended solution. Plotting means taking the range and bearing of other targets at frequent intervals and plotting them on special plotting sheets. To these plots you then apply the course and speed of your own vessel which enables you to

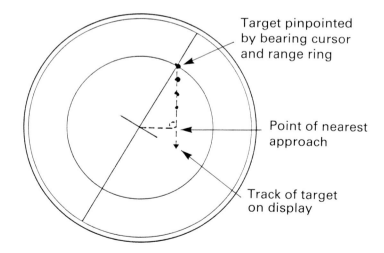

Target pinpointed by bearing cursor and range ring

Point of nearest approach

Track of target on display

Tracking an approaching target on the radar. The first position is fixed by the intersection of the range ring and bearing line. The closest approach is shown by the imaginary line at right angles to the line joining successive target positions. If the bearing does not change a great deal then you are on, or close to, a collision course.

complete the vector triangle to find out the course and speed of the other vessel. This type of plotting is not something you have much chance of carrying out on board a fast boat at sea, so you must look for other techniques to comply with collision avoidance requirements. Some of them can be used on the radar but others can be the basis of your navigation technique in fog.

First, anything you can do to reduce the number of other vessels you have to cope with in poor visibility will help the situation. This applies particularly to large ships which, because of their size and poor manoeuvrability, you will not want to tangle with in fog. You cannot actually get rid of the ships – they have as much right to be there as you have – but you can keep away from them. Ships tend to follow set courses between harbours and ports, and although in the open sea their movements may appear to be more random it is possible to set your course to avoid the obvious shipping lanes. At sea you may have to cross these main routes, in which case you should try and do so at right angles to cross in the shortest possible time; it could also be prudent to wait until you see a gap in the ships showing on the radar screen before crossing. Your high speed can give you an advantage here to keep clear of other vessels, which may not be open to slower craft.

When you are travelling along the coast other shipping will probably be doing the same thing, but in general it will keep at least two miles off headlands. In a small, fast craft you are quite safe to pass much closer provided, of course, there are no offlying dangers or tide races. Even if there are such features the ships will usually allow a generous safety margin around the headlands leaving you clear room to make an inside passage.

Once around the headland the ships will make a straight course for the next one. This is the shortest distance and time is money to them. If you set your course slightly into the bay, then you should keep clear of all the shipping. Another point to remember is that ships generally have a fairly deep draft, certainly in comparison with the average fast boat, so there are many areas of shallow water which are quite safe for small craft but to which ships will give a wide berth. Again you may have to go out of your way a little to make use of some of these, but the increased peace of mind makes it worthwhile and you may be able to make better speeds.

The same applies when you are entering harbour or using buoyed channels. The buoys are generally laid to mark the deep water channel which is for the use of shipping. Almost invariably there is an area of shallow water outside the main channel which is perfectly suitable for small craft. Even if you want to hop from buoy to buoy in the channel to keep a check on your position by visual observation you can do this on the other side of the buoys from the deep water channel, where you should have a reasonably clear path as far as other vessels are concerned. Another advantage of this technique is that if you do see the water shoaling too much on your echo sounder, you will have no doubt as to which way to turn to find deeper water.

When entering harbour there will come a time when you probably will have to mix with the big ships, but fog usually restricts the movements of these vessels in harbour much more than it will for small craft. There should be no difficulty here and even if you do meet big shipping in enclosed waters it will be moving very slowly, and so hopefully will you. The only exception here may be ferry boats which have a habit of ploughing along at full speed irrespective of visibility; the only consolation you can take here is that these craft tend to follow regular tracks which can often be identified from the chart, and that the ferries know the waters well and will almost certainly be aware of your presence. To make sure they are not taken unawares, you should proceed at moderate or slow speed in their vicinity so that both they and you can cope with the situation.

One point to remember when you are entering harbour is that you may need time to clarify the situation. The radar picture can change rapidly and there may be several targets ahead of which you are not sure. If this is the case then stop and work things out rather than rush on and hope that the situation will clarify itself. If there are tidal streams then it is always better to enter harbour on the ebb tide because this means that if you do need to stop to take stock for any reason you will not be carried forward into an unwelcome situation but

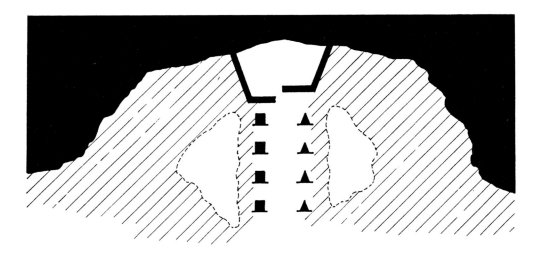

The clear areas in the main channel show where big ships will navigate, leaving the rest of the area for small craft. There is a space for small craft to navigate just outside the main channel buoys to avoid shipping, and ships are unlikely to pass into the bay or close round headlands.

will be able to keep control whilst stemming the tide. Stemming the tide also enables you to stop in relation to the ground whilst still maintaining your craft on a heading. This will help to keep the radar picture steady, something which can be very important when entering harbour. If the boat swings then all the targets on the radar display will also swing and create a very confused picture for a while, probably just at the time when you want it clear. There is no doubt that an autopilot can be very useful for maintaining a stable picture in this situation, but it should be one that has a rapid disconnect button if you need to take manual control in a hurry.

Returning to the general techniques for collision avoidance in fast craft, what you need to know from the information on the display is which of the approaching targets you can safely ignore because they present no danger, and which ones you should be concerned about and need more information on. Any targets which are moving away from the centre of the screen on a relative motion display will be moving away from you and need not concern you. Any moving towards the centre or at some point near the centre are those you need to keep a very close eye on.

There are two classic ways of pinpointing what the targets on the screen are doing in relation to you. One is to put the VBM (variable bearing marker) on the target, averaging out its position if your boat is swinging about a little under manual helm. If after a minute or two the bearing has not changed appreciably and the target still lies on the VBM line, then there is a risk of collision if you both maintain your course and speed. By also putting the VRM (variable range marker) on the target at the same time you will be able to appreciate how rapidly the other vessel is closing with yours and will know whether immediate action is called for or whether you have time to take more checks. If your radar has two VRMs and VBMs you can leave one set on the original position of the target and the second set on the new position, so that you will have some idea of the relative motion of the target. It is not too difficult in this situation mentally to apply your course and speed to find out just what the approximate course and speed of the other vessel might be. Your course and speed vector will be parallel to the heading marker, applied from the point where the target was first plotted.

With twin VRMs and VBMs you can also keep track of two targets at once, which is probably a more valuable use of this feature. Certainly in terms of the bearing cursor any change in the bearing tends to be welcome; if the bearing opens up on the bow then the other vessel should pass to that side of you, but if it closes towards the ahead position then the vessel should pass ahead of you, always assuming that both of you and they maintain course and speed.

You may well think this is all the information required to find out what the other vessel is doing, but there are other points to remember. Bearings can often be unreliable on a small fast craft, particularly if the heading is swinging about. This may make it difficult to get a good reliable assessment of any change in bearing. Another point to consider is just how much of a change in bearing is required before it can be counted as safe. A vessel approaching on a reciprocal course will only change its bearing very, very slowly at first, yet it may still pass a mile away when it is abeam. Conversely a vessel approaching on the bow will change its bearing quite rapidly and yet may not pass a great distance away from you. In the case of the vessel approaching from ahead the bearing will only start to alter appreciably once the range has been closed considerably. This emphasises the need to watch the bearing all the time as up till now we have been assuming that the approaching vessel has been maintaining a steady course and speed. Any change in either of these factors will affect the bearing. In this situation it is important to put yourself in the position of the person in charge of the other vessel. They may have picked up the target of your craft on their radar and decided that the two vessels are on a collision course, prompting them to alter course to avoid such a situation.

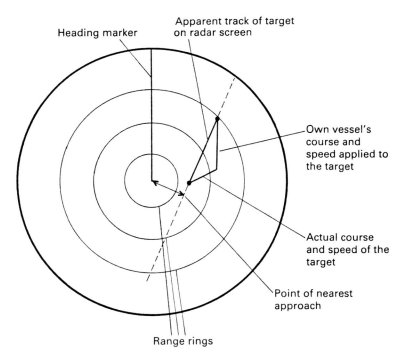

Using a relative motion radar it is possible to work out the actual course and speed of an approaching vessel.

Only constant watching of the bearing will determine this — and then only some time after the alteration has been made.

It is in a situation such as this when vessels are approaching from ahead or nearly ahead that the parallel index lines can be quite valuable. If you put the VBM on the ahead or zero mark the parallel index lines will be parallel to your course; it is then much easier to judge whether the other vessel is edging towards you, moving away or, as a third alternative, approaching parallel to your course. You will be able to spot any changes much more rapidly as the target moves towards or away from one of the parallel index lines. Another useful radar feature is a wandering VBM and VRM. You can put the datum point on the target when it is first sighted and line the VBM on the subsequent appearances of the target. This line will then show how close the target will pass you if both of you maintain course and speed.

Making any alteration of course or speed to avoid a collision can only be achieved with any degree of safety by carrying out plotting procedures but, as we have seen, this is not really feasible in a small fast craft. Unless you have a very good reason you are better to maintain your course and speed to avoid confusing other vessels and this will also maintain your radar picture in a more readily understandable format. One of the problems with many small boats now being fitted with radar is that there tends to be a lot of undisciplined manoeuvring of these craft in poor visibility, resulting in confusion. Maintaining your course and speed will help you to maintain control of the situation. Any alteration in your course or speed will be reflected in the behaviour of the targets on your display and the steadier you can keep this the more fully you will be in control of events.

One of the prime objects of plotting is to determine the point of nearest approach of the other vessel. If two positions of the echo from the vessel are plotted the extended line joining them will show how close the two vessels will pass provided both maintain their present courses and speeds. You can carry out this type of plotting operation mentally on the radar screen by marking the initial position of the vessel with the bearing cursor and the VRM. After a suitable time interval it is then possible to join this line to the new position of the target by an imaginary line and get some idea of the point of nearest approach. Radars with a wandering point VBM and VRM can be useful to link up plotted positions to give a much clearer indication of the point of nearest approach. Another method of tracking targets is by means of a persistent tail, which is a historical track of the target retained on the screen and a feature found on some radars.

By keeping out of the shipping lanes you can hopefully reduce the number of targets you have to deal with on the screen. By using one of the above methods you can also eliminate some of the others, although they should still be watched closely in case they start to act unpredictably, perhaps taking avoiding action for another target which may be near them. This system should help simplify your work and enable you to concentrate on those targets which refuse to keep clear – hopefully you will only have to deal with one of these at a time.

At what range you should start to show real concern at an approaching vessel depends on many factors. The range of visibility is one, but do not depend on this remaining constant. Speed and manoeuvrability of your craft are other factors, and on high speed craft these are usually working in your favour. The type of approaching vessel is the third aspect, but this is not something that you can readily identify, although you may have some idea whether it is a fast or slow vessel by the relative speed at which the target is approaching.

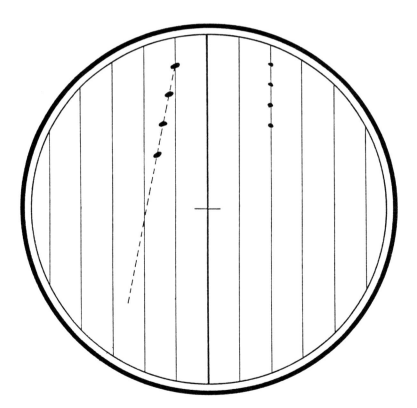

Parallel indexing lines on the radar screen can make it much easier to work out the track of an approaching vessel or the distance you would pass off a headland. The target on the right is on a parallel course, whilst the target on the left is moving away.

Any vessel approaching to within one mile should give you cause for concern and you should consider taking action at this point. The logical course is to stop the engines. This serves the dual purpose of buying time and giving you silence to listen for the fog signal of the approaching vessel. Rather than stop completely, however, it is better just to slow down in order to keep the picture stabilised; once again operating with an autopilot will achieve this much better than manual control. Certainly a close-quarter situation is not one where you want the radar picture going round in circles, which is a good reason for not stopping the engines completely. At this point a close watch should be kept on the display and the bearing of the approaching vessel checked continually. In many circumstances a change in speed will be sufficient to enable the two craft to pass clear if they were on a collision course.

This is the time to start concentrating on your visual lookout and you will know roughly the direction from which the vessel is approaching. There is nothing quite like a visual sighting to enable you to take positive action to avoid collision, and provided you have a few hundred yards visibility then you should be able to take such action in good time after a visual sighting has been made.

It is often possible to identify large ships on the radar screen, particularly when they are close, simply by the size of the target. Here your technique could well be different because you don't want to get too close to these large ships. Some cannot even see their bow when the visibility is down to, say, 300 yards, and yet in small craft this could give you more than enough space to do a complete turn or come to a halt. You are certainly best advised to keep well clear of large ships, even if in theory it is their job to give way. They may be restricted as to how they can manoeuvre by adjacent shallow water, so if you can identify a large ship, alter course and steer well clear of it, making the alteration of course positive so that it will be aware of what you are doing and not be concerned about your movements.

In any situation in fog there is always a risk that both vessels approaching on collision courses will take action by altering course and speed at the same time, in fact worsening the situation rather than solving it. This is why it is always best to use a reduction in speed rather than an alteration of course, which will succeed in buying time to sort out the situation and also conform to the rules of the road.

In a fast boat, because of the tremendous speed difference between you and most other vessels on the water, you have an additional option open to you: to treat all the other targets on the radar screen virtually as vessels which are stopped, so that you steer your way round them. This course of action does contravene the regulations but no one is likely to argue with it provided you don't have a collision. However, if you do adopt this course then you must make sure that you steer well clear of all the other craft and not cause the utmost panic by zooming close by them. You can only adopt this technique if you are travelling at speeds of 40 knots or more, and it could be argued that this is an unsafe speed to use in fog, but I have used this technique in low visibility and it certainly enables you to make good progress provided you concentrate totally on the job that you are doing and work within the limitations of your radar. For this sort of operation you certainly want a good quality radar and it is not a technique I would recommend in narrow channels where your ability to manoeuvre might well be limited.

In general then, navigating in fog is certainly not something to undertake lightly. Neither is it a job for one person trying to steer the boat, watch the radar and keep a lookout. If you are going to navigate successfully and carry out collision avoidance at high speed then you need one person to concentrate solely on the lookout, one to concentrate solely on the radar, and another to steer and monitor the progress of the vessel. As we have already said, steering by autopilot has its advantages in fog and could release one person for other work, but whichever division of duties you adopt concentration is still vital. The radar screen should certainly have undivided attention, not only to keep a track of what the targets are doing, but also to watch for that unexpected small target that may appear at close quarters.

Rain is unlikely to occur with fog and so you should not have the associated problems detecting targets, but fog itself, particularly when it is damp, can reduce the penetration of the radar beam and this may reduce the detection level of targets. Sea clutter probably represents the worst problem in fog because this can mean that you lose small boat targets just at a time when you need to know where they are and what they are doing. The only solution here is to adjust carefully the level of the clutter setting to find the right balance between reduction of clutter and detection of targets. Fortunately the combination of fog and rough seas is less frequent, so clutter is not usually a major problem.

If you want to navigate with confidence in fog then you do need a high quality radar. Many small boat radars with their poor bearing and range discrimination and their small displays and lack of facilities are not really adequate for these conditions. If navigating in fog is vital to the performance of the craft, as it can be with patrol and pilot boats and other commercial craft, then the best quality radar that can be fitted to the vessel is the requirement. It would be rare for a full ARPA radar to be feasible because of its high cost and size but such a radar does all the plotting electronically for you on the screen and takes a lot of guesswork out of collision avoidance.

Most of the plotting work done by ARPA radars is achieved by complex software and there really is no reason why such software cannot be introduced to radars for smaller craft – but this is a development for the future and would increase the cost of radars considerably. An option found on some radars today, as discussed above, enables the targets to 'remember' their previous tracks on the screen by a tail which extends from the target in the direction in which it has travelled. This can be very helpful for collision avoidance because it gives you some idea of the relative course and speed of targets on the screen and you can't use the bearing and range markers to plot all their positions.

To use radar effectively in fog it has to be constantly monitored and you need ready access to the controls. This is where separate controls and display really come in useful.

12 Navigating with the weather

To a fast powerboat the weather conditions are just as important as they are for a sailing yacht. The weather can dictate your tactics and your speed just as it does for yachts under sail, but the main difference is that a powerboat has a much greater capacity to dictate where you are in relation to the weather, which puts you in the unique position of being at least partly in control of the weather situation. You could have the speed to outrun or overtake the weather or you could accelerate the passage of a front as you drive through it. Most weather is time critical, and by combining or subtracting your speed from the speed at which the weather moves you have an element of control. This ability to 'play' the weather in a fast boat emphasises the need to fully understand the weather and the way it behaves.

It is not so much the weather that interests you, but rather the effects of the wind on the water. Wind on its own will only have a small effect on your progress but the waves it generates can have a profound effect on the performance of a fast boat. These waves in turn are affected by tides and currents, by shallow water and by the land. Combinations of conditions can generate local disturbances in the sea which can be dangerous to fast boats, and the way sea conditions change when the tide turns in some areas highlights the need for a full understanding of the weather situation and its effects.

Consideration of the weather is thus a vital part of the navigation of a fast boat and it will help formulate and decide your tactics. Because of your speed you have much more flexibility in terms of tactics, so the shortest route may not always be the fastest. Just setting a course and following it regardless of the weather is the easy option as far as fast boat navigation is concerned, but you shouldn't ignore what the weather is trying to tell you.

WEATHER FORECASTS

Weather forecasts today are generally very accurate except for one aspect – timing. The forecast will give you an accurate portrayal of the weather situation, showing the areas of high and low pressure and the associated fronts. Successive forecasts should give you some idea of how the lows and fronts are moving, but you need something better – something which will give you more accurate timing in your particular locality. The reason is that it is usually the arrival of a front or the movement of a low which heralds changes in the wind. These changes can be important to you, particularly changes in wind direction and strength. Armed with detailed knowledge of the changes you can plan your tactics with a degree of confidence and take maximum advantage of what the weather has to offer. Of course, if you do your boating in an area with consistent weather then you needn't be so concerned, but even these areas tend to have isolated weather changes which arrive at short notice, so it pays to keep a weather eye open.

Given generally accurate forecasts, how can we improve the timing? You have to remember that forecasters are usually producing charts for general rather than specific areas. They have the information to be specific, but most forecasts on TV or radio cover a large area and forecasters have to be all things to all men. Now if you can talk to the forecasters directly, discussing the areas of specific interest to you, then in most cases they will be able to come up with a specific forecast to meet your requirement. They may still be reticent about the timing, but if so it is because they genuinely don't know and this in turn should make you a little cautious. In most areas there is a facility for talking direct to a forecaster, so seek one out; it is worth paying a little extra to have your own specific forecast. Information about where to contact a forecaster can usually be found in telephone directories or from harbour masters or marina controllers.

Arm yourself with a weather map before calling. This will give you the general weather picture and you will be in a much better position to appreciate what you are being told if you can relate it to the map. The other requirement is a basic knowledge of weather patterns and their associated frontal systems if you want a fuller understanding of what is going on. Any of the good yachting weather books will give you the grounding you need, and as you gain experience you will be able to out-guess the forecasters.

In these days of instant weather forecasts we have become lazy about understanding the weather. However, when you are concerned about the timing and significance of changes, a vital ingredient in the picture can be provided by your own observations. Once you understand the way fronts are formed you will be able to see where you are in relation to an approaching front and probably have just as good an idea of when changes can be expected as the forecaster. The important thing is to gather information from all the sources at your disposal, but remember at the end of the day that what you do in regard to the weather is your decision and it doesn't help to turn round and blame the forecast. The weather signs are there for those who want to see them.

STRATEGIC WEATHER PLANNING

Here I refer to your planning with regard to the weather forecast and the way weather features are moving. In a fast boat you have much more flexibility in this respect, even to the point of running before the weather or overtaking it. The weather patterns are rarely static and it is the changes that you are concerned with. In a fast boat you are in a much better position to take advantage of any changes or to complete a voyage before they arrive.

It is the weather fronts which tend to bring the more sudden changes in the weather, otherwise the winds swing gradually round one way or the other. In fronts the wind change can be quite dramatic, up to 90 degrees in some cases, and such a change can have a considerable bearing on your strategy, particularly when the winds are quite fresh. With such a change, what would be sheltered waters could become exposed or vice versa. Fronts travel at different speeds and directions so you need as much information as possible for your planning, but a front will rarely move at more than 30–40 knots so in a fast boat you should be able to remain in control of the situation.

There are a variety of ways you can exploit your speed potential. First, if you want to travel in the same direction as a front which is bringing stronger winds with it then you can get out to sea in good time and run before it. You may be able to do this even though the forecast doesn't sound very hopeful, but do bear in mind that if you have an engine problem the bad weather could soon catch up with you. You could use a similar tactic if a front has just gone through taking the good weather with it. Here it might pay to put up with a little discomfort and push the boat hard in the early stages in the knowledge that you will be running into better weather as you overtake the front. You might also want to alter course to pass through the front at right angles to its direction of travel to get through as quickly as possible. The winds tend to blow in the direction in which the front is travelling, so in these manoeuvres you will tend to have a following sea which will help your speed.

Going to windward will involve taking the frontal system head on, but your speed combined with that of the front will mean that you get through it quickly. There can also be periods in the passage of a front when the wind eases for a short while, usually when it is changing direction; you can take advantage of such a lull to make a short passage. Additionally there is often a lull in the wind at dawn and dusk – particularly at dawn – which can again give you the chance to make a passage of 20 or 30 miles before the wind freshens.

In these situations look out for the effects of land (daytime) and sea breezes (night-time) when these local winds caused by the heating or cooling of the land can increase or reduce the general wind pattern. Also beware of the way the wind can increase where it is funnelled around a headland. This type of local wind can make conditions worse in an area where tides and other factors are already adverse effects on the waves.

On a coastal passage it is the headlands which can be barriers to your progress. Once you are round a headland there is a choice of options which can be used to improve progress. At the headland the choices are limited unless there is an inside passage, but planning to arrive at slack water or at dawn can give you a better chance of finding the right conditions.

In strategic weather planning there are no hard and fast rules. I am a great believer in going out and having a look to see what the conditions are like rather than listening to the advice of harbour experts or the information from general forecasts. There is a general lack of understanding about the capabilities of fast boats in bad conditions, and the fact that a fast boat can make a passage in one hour which would take a displacement boat four or five hours. If you go out and have a look you will be able to relate what you find with what you know about the weather patterns and can make up your mind. Try not to take things to the limits, always keep something in reserve in case things don't work out as planned – and don't be afraid to turn back if you don't like what you see. The trip out of the harbour will have been valuable experience even if you haven't reached where you wanted to go.

EFFECTS OF WIND ON THE SEA

Up to force 3 the effect of the wind on the sea will not worry you too much. The waves will not be high enough to affect your speed even in the fastest of boats, although there may be an underlying swell which could cause more concern. Above this wind speed, the waves will start to build rapidly in size and this could have a profound effect on your navigation tactics. A great deal will depend on the direction of the wind in relation to that in which you want to travel; the other aspect to consider is fetch.

Fetch is the distance between your position and the nearest land upwind. It is significant because the wave size increases the further offshore you are downwind from the shore. With the wind blowing off the land, you will find sheltered water close inshore because the wind has only a slight effect on the sea here where the waves have not had time to build up in size. A couple of miles offshore you will see the wave size start to increase, perhaps enough to slow you down, whilst ten miles off the waves will start to reach full height for the particular wind strength.

The effect of fetch can be used to advantage when you are running along a coastline. If you draw a line on the chart in the direction from which the wind is coming you will see the distance or fetch over which the wind can build up the waves. The greater the fetch, the higher the waves. This line transferred along the coastline will also show you areas where you can expect to find shelter. As the wind becomes stronger so the size of the waves in any particular area will increase. In strong winds the extent of the sheltered areas will be reduced if you take a particular wave height as the yardstick. There are tables to show the expected wave height with a given wind strength and fetch, but these are mainly for ocean rather than coastal waters. Some forecasts will give wave height for coastal waters but these are averages; tides, currents, shallow water and the land all complicate the picture.

FACTORS AFFECTING WAVES

The tide probably has the most dramatic affect on the waves. When the tide is running in the same direction as the wind the wave length is effectively increased. This means that the gradient of the wave is reduced and it will look far less threatening. The gradient of a wave is the main factor which affects fast boat performance, so the reduced gradient will be welcome and can be a significant factor in speed of progress.

The reverse happens when the wind is against the tide. The wave gradient is steepened, having a corresponding adverse effect on the performance of a fast boat. The effect of the change in tidal direction will depend a great deal on the strength of the tide. A tide of under 1 knot will have a noticeable but not significant effect on the waves except in stronger winds, say over force 5. With tides of 3 knots a change in tidal direction can have a dramatic effect on the sea conditions, changing a sea which is moderate and which allows good progress into one where there can be steep breaking crests to the waves, and progress at any speed can be difficult.

Currents can have the same effect on the waves as tidal streams – the Gulf Stream of Florida is a good example. The main difference, of course, is that the current doesn't change direction so the conditions will remain consistent with the wind strength. With tides the danger lies in the changes itself. In some sea areas the tidal stream can change direction without much alteration in strength – the change in sea conditions can then be sudden and dramatic. You should not contemplate navigating a fast boat without knowing what the tides are doing – or more importantly, what the tidal streams are doing.

Shallow water has the well known effect of making waves break and these conditions with larger waves can be found in waters deep enough for fast boat navigation. It can be worse if a tidal stream is hitting the shallow water causing the flow to be upset. Here there can be local disturbances which may change position and strength with the change in tide.

You can export to find sheltered later in the lee of shallow water, which at least will filter out the larger waves. Much will depend on the depth of the water on the shoal and the extent of the shoal so don't count on finding sheltered water behind small shoals; indeed you could find worse conditions due to

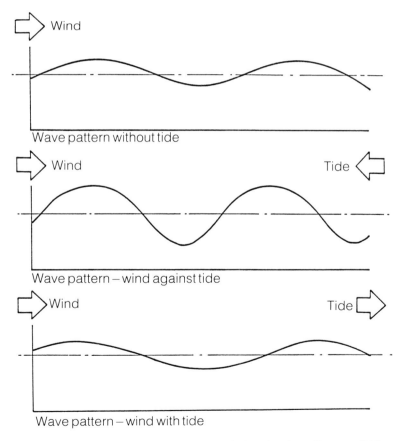

The way in which the wave profile is modified under the influence of tides or currents.

refraction. This is where the waves are slowed down in shallow water causing the wave form to change direction, so you can end up with crossing wave trains behind a shoal. The same can happen behind an island, and indeed refraction can also cause problems round headlands, continuing rough seas where you might expect to find shelter. You will find the shelter eventually, but you will have to go further round the headland to find it.

So far we have looked at all these factors more or less in isolation, but it is generally combinations of the different factors that create nasty situations. A tidal stream sweeping round a pronounced headland can generate a tide race with its associated dangers. Tides or currents forced through narrow channels between islands and the mainland can have the same effect, and you only need to add a little shallow water to make things worse. On top of this you have to consider the effect of the wind, and if it is blowing against the tide you have conditions which are not good for fast boats – or any boat for that matter.

Headlands and islands are obviously places where you can expect to find difficult conditions. The chart and pilot books will identify the worst of these areas, but you still need to make your own interpretation of what effect the prevailing wind will have. There is one redeeming feature about some headlands which is that you can sometimes find a relatively calm water passage close to the headland which can help you escape from the worst of the seas. Such inside passages are only viable if there are no rocks or shoals off the headland and even then you need care to negotiate them. These inside passages are only possible at certain headlands and information about them may be hard to find except from local knowledge. To negotiate them you often have to head for a point inside the headland and then follow the coast closely round and up the other side before resuming your course.

Given experience, it is possible to study the chart and the tide tables and come up with an estimation of what the sea conditions will be like along the route you propose to follow, bearing in mind what wind is forecast. This should be part of your preparatory work and it is a good idea to shade in areas on the chart where you expect difficult sea conditions. There are many factors to take into account when working this out which is why experience is helpful, but at least by doing so you will help prevent nasty surprises during the passage.

Many weather forecasts also give an indication of the wave height, and in areas where there is little or no tide such as the Mediterranean this can be useful information. In other areas the tremendous variation in wave height and gradient which can be generated in local areas makes such information of doubtful value and it could give you a false sense of security. Perhaps one day computers will be able to take all the factors into account to assess sea conditions on a continuous basis, but at present you have to do this for yourself and relate them to how they will affect your boat and its performance. This is a vital part of fast boat navigation and will play a large part in deciding the tactics you adopt for making a passage.

WEATHER TACTICS

The weather and sea conditions play a larger part in fast boat navigation than with most other craft. The sea conditions will affect your speed of progress quite considerably so that the shortest distance will not always be the fastest. You often see this in offshore racing where a deviation from the straight course of say two or three miles is well worthwhile if it allows you to increase speed by 10 knots over a 30 mile run. The same holds true for a fast pleasure boat or a patrol boat. Not only will you be able to make a faster passage if you seek out the calmer sea conditions, but life on board will also be much more comfortable with less strain on boat and crew.

When planning your weather tactics the main condition that you want to avoid is a head sea. Nothing slows a boat down more than head seas, particularly when they are short and steep, and you will also want to avoid the local areas of disturbed water already mentioned from whatever direction they come. There are various ways of avoiding head seas; the most obvious is to run in sheltered water where the wave height will not be significant enough to affect performance. A study of the chart will show where you might expect to find sheltered water which will keep the head seas down to a size which will not affect performance unduly.

You are unlikely to find sheltered water where you want it, so the alternative is to alter course so that the seas are not approaching from directly ahead. Altering course in this way has the effect of reducing the speed of encounter with the waves, so that you will tend to have a more comfortable ride and be able to increase speed. It is rather like tacking in a sailboat because you can't travel upwind.

'Tacking' in this way is not likely to get you to your destination any faster if that direction is directly upwind. You will need to alter course at least 30 degrees to have a noticeable effect on performance, and the extra distance you have to cover will be barely compensated by your extra speed. If time is not critical, the improved comfort could make such a tactic worthwhile – but remember that you could get the same benefit simply by slowing down.

Perhaps the main value of 'tacking' in this way is that, by doing so, the new course may take you into calmer water. This can best be appreciated by considering a typical bay where you are making a passage from one headland to the next. If the wind is directly ahead there will be no shelter and you will have a rough passage across the bay. Now if you 'tack' into the bay you will first have the benefit of the wind on the bow rather than dead ahead for the first part of the crossing, which will improve the ride. Once you get into the bay you will start to feel the benefit of the shelter from the land because the fetch will be reduced, and the last part of your crossing will be in almost calm water. You will still hit rough seas when you round the headland but there might be a calmer inside passage. The extra distance in this case will be repaid by higher speeds and a better ride.

A similar situation can occur if the wind is blowing off the land. With a wide bay the sea conditions in the middle could be quite nasty with a fetch of several miles. Even though the wind is on the beam this could give a faster passage. Another reason for heading inside a bay is that the tides are generally weaker here so that any wind against tide situation will not have such a pronounced effect.

These sort of deviations from the direct course can be part of your planning tactics, but there are also short-term tactics which you can adopt. It's always worth trying an alteration of 10 or 20 degrees from the direct course to see what effect it has on the ride. In a following sea, even though you are overtaking the waves, a small alteration can make quite a difference. Try to view any such alteration in the longer term because you can usually derive the

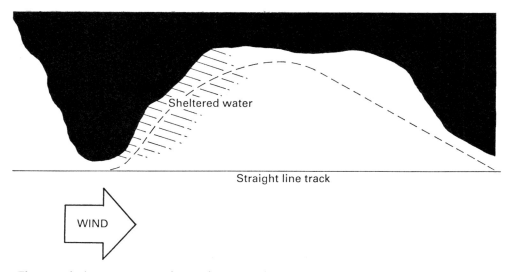

The straight line course into the wind gives you head winds all the way, but by deviating into the bay you not only put the wind 30° on the bow, but also have sheltered water as you cross the bay.

same benefit in the short term from altering to either side of the course. You need to see from which side you will gain most benefit as you approach your destination.

It is always worth trying small course alterations if you find the conditions becoming uncomfortable. A particular example is when the wind is on the bow and it picks up the spray and directs it straight in your face; here a small alteration of course may make all the difference. Changes of speed can also be beneficial when conditions are uncomfortable and here it is worth bearing in mind that slowing down is not always the best solution. Opening the throttles can sometimes get the boat up on top of the waves, particularly if you control the trim carefully, and you can make much better progress.

These changes of course and speed can upset your navigation planning, so think about the effect on navigation before you finally decide. Heading into the land should not cause you any problems provided the visibility is good or you have radar. It helps to know some identifying features on the land you approach so that you can check your progress. Heading away from the land can be more difficult; here you will have to rely on timing to know when to head back in again. With electronic position fixing you can keep a check on progress in relation to the original track by watching the cross track error; naturally the course and distance to the next waypoint will help you get to where you want to go.

SEEKING SHELTER

Even in the best organised boat things can go wrong. You may have an engine failure bringing you down to a slow speed, the weather might prove worse than you expected so that you find bad sea conditions. On most fast boat passages you should have sufficient margins to cope, but occasionally you may be tempted to cut things a little fine, and at the back of your mind you should have an idea of what to do if things go wrong. From a navigation point of view this means having an idea of what alternative harbours might be available or where you might at least go to find calmer water to perhaps carry out engine repairs.

Harbours are the obvious solution if things go wrong and you should in any case have some idea of what harbours might be available along your route. Some may have tidal limitations or lack the sort of facilities needed for a fast boat. Possibly the main worry will be conditions in the harbour entrance. The very conditions outside in the open sea which are causing you to seek shelter could also generate difficult and perhaps dangerous seas at the entrance, which could make entering harbour more risky even than staying out at sea.

The sort of harbour conditions which could spell trouble are those where the wind is blowing towards the shore, where the ebb tide is running out of the harbour and where there is shallow water in the entrance. This combination will almost certainly generate a dangerous breaking sea in the entrance, a sea made more dangerous because, coming in from seaward, you will probably not realise just how bad it is until you get amongst the breaking waves. In daylight you might be able to cope – probably the best solution is to run in at planing speeds so that you are running at the same speed as the waves or overtaking them. (You must of course slow down once inside to conform to harbour speed limits.) At night such a situation can be very dangerous indeed because you can't see what is going on.

If you want to enter a harbour for shelter then it can help if you speak to the harbour authorities ashore by radio. This will give you a much better idea of the conditions and facilities and will help you make up your mind whether to attempt an entry. I would suggest that if you have any doubts it is better to stay

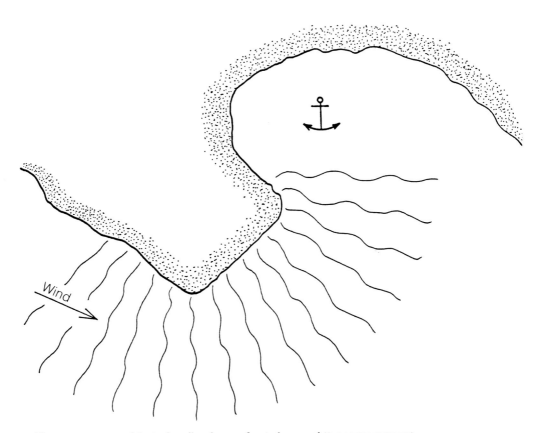

The waves approaching a headland are refracted around it, so you may not always find shelter where you expect it.

outside, but it is easy to say that without having to suffer the discomfort of remaining at sea. What is important is to try to be objective about the decision.

An alternative to entering harbour is to tuck in under a headland or other area where there is protection from the wind and the seas it can generate. Headlands do not always give the protection they promise because of the refraction of the waves, and you will need to tuck yourself close in under the land to get good shelter. Even then there can be a ground swell which can make life uncomfortable when you anchor, but it should be better than taking the full force of wind and tide. Keep a close watch on the forecast when sheltering in this way, because if the wind changes direction your sheltered area could change into a rough patch and you may be worse off in the long term.

THE WEATHER AND FAST BOATS

Fast boat navigation is not simply a matter of plotting courses and using electronics. The weather and its effect on sea conditions plays a vital role and you cannot navigate a fast boat without considering them. These are the limiting factors in the boat's progress, so to be a successful fast boat navigator you also have to be a meteorologist and understand what the effect of the weather might be. At high speed, as we have seen, you have much more flexibility to negotiate the weather and you have more options open to you than you would in a slow boat.

To understand these options you need an alert mind, but the fast boat environment is not conducive to rational thought. This means that navigation has to start on the drawing board, to create a boat and an environment which will give you the best chance of coping with the difficult conditions. From there you need to prepare your navigation as much as possible before you go, but this can never eliminate the need to make decisions on the spot as you go along. You can find yourself in a fast changing situation where a variety of factors relating to sea conditions, your position, the course, all have to be assessed to find the optimum solution. This is where experience counts.

Modern navigation electronics can help a great deal by producing answers to many of the problems and one day they may become sophisticated enough to assess the sea conditions too. Then we will be moving well down the road to automation, but until that day experience will be a vital factor in fast boat navigation. This book will, hopefully, put you on the right track, but it is only by going out to sea and gaining practical experience that you will become a competent fast boat navigator.

Other Adlard Coles titles of interest

Fast Boats and Rough Seas: Dag Pike
    ISBN 0   229   11840   2
This book is designed to explain advanced
handling techniques for fast boats. Topics
covered include an analysis of how waves are
formed and their effect on the boat, hull
shape as related to speed and seaworthiness,
controlling the boat, crew comfort,
navigation under difficult conditions, power
requirements, equipment and fittings for
high speed and emergency procedures. This
very practical book will be greatly welcomed
by fast boat skippers and crew.

Marine Inboard Engines (Petrol and Diesel):
Loris Goring
    ISBN   0   229   11842   9
This handy volume will enable every owner to
maintain their diesel or petrol engine to
maximise its life span and avoid breakdown
at sea. It answers such questions as: What
should you look for when buying a used
engine? Is an air cooled engine necessarily
noisier than water cooled? How do electronic
ignition systems work? It is designed to give
the newcomer to boating an insight into the
workings of a boat engine and at the same
time cater for the older hand who wishes to
learn more. Goring gives sound advice and
guidance as to which jobs the amateur can
safely undertake and which should be left to
the professional engineer.

Channel Crossings For Power and Sail:
Peter Cumberlidge
    ISBN   0   229   11852   6
An invaluable reference book for anyone
planning to set off for foreign waters. It is a
completely new style of passage-making
guide for over 16 open sea routes starting
from popular ports around the coast of
Britain. For each crossing the author gives
pilotage and navigational details; guidance
on waypoints, tidal streams, weather
forecasts, optimum times of departure and
arrival and suggests tactics for poor visibility
and heavy weather.

Using Your Decca: Pat Langley-Price and
Philip Ouvry
    ISBN   0   229   11853   4
This book aims to help owners get the best
from their sets and make full use of the
facilities offered, from waypoint selection to
the man overboard facility, as well as fully
appreciating Decca's limitations.

Reading the Weather: Alan Watts
    ISBN 0   229   11774   0
Weather forecasting has entered a new age of
sophistication based on the introduction of
satellite information and computer
technology. These new techniques need
explanation and as new forecasting
hardware becomes cheaper, items such as
'weather fax' will become common aboard
and wherever the elements are important to
business or pleasure. This definitive work
will be of great interest to all seafarers.